The Website. The Book.

BY **The Writers of CollegeHumor**

EDITED BY **Streeter Seidell**
Jeff Rubin
Susanna Wolff

ILLUSTRATED BY **Caldwell Tanner**

DESIGNED BY **Amir Cohen**
Derek Winegar

Da Capo Press
A Member of the Perseus Books Group

DISCLAIMER: We can't imagine that anyone in their right mind would think that people, companies, products, publications or cartoon characters depicted in this book have any affiliation with us or necessarily approve of their appearance in this book. However, we also believe that many people are not in their right mind. Specifically, the lawyers representing the people, companies, products, publications or cartoon characters depicted in this book. They could persuade themselves to believe that someone could mistakenly confuse the humorous works herein with the very serious works of their clients. So, to the lawyers representing Facebook, Mark Zuckerberg, Batman, Google, Denny's, Chuck E. Cheese, Apple, Home Depot and anyone else who (sort of) appears within, we hope you're enjoying your bathroom break! We also hope you'll see that this is all a joke. Nobody is going to confuse your client's work with ours.

FURTHER DISCLAIMER: This book will be extremely hot if lit on fire.

Cataloging-in-Publication data for this book is available from the Library of Congress.

First Da Capo Press edition 2011

ISBN: 978-0-306-82026-7

E-Book ISBN: 978-0-306-82049-6

Published by Da Capo Press
A Member of the Perseus Books Group
www.dacapopress.com

Da Capo Press books are available at special discounts for bulk purchases in the U.S. by corporations, institutions, and other organizations. For more information, please contact the Special Markets Department at the Perseus Books Group, 2300 Chestnut Street, Suite 200, Philadelphia, PA 19103, or call (800) 810-4145, ext. 5000, or e-mail special.markets@perseusbooks.com.

10 9 8 7 6 5 4 3 2 1

Contents

Introduction

Congratulations! You've bought a book. And not just any book, you've bought a book of previously published material, which means you're either a big fan of ours or a sucker. Either way, we thank you kindly.

So what will you find in this book? Inspiration, perhaps? A purpose, even! But more likely, you will find a collection of our staff's favorite articles from the founding of the website in 1999 until we rushed to turn in this manuscript in 2011. They are not organized in any way, though they do have one thing in common: they are funny. Or, at least, we think they are funny. From sublimely subtle satires to pieces without a single instance of alliteration, the articles in this book run the gamut (which we imagine to be some sort of medieval initiation ritual). Whether you enjoy insightful essays, colorful comics, or Photoshopped Facebook newsfeeds, we have you covered. Especially if you enjoy Photoshopped Facebook newsfeeds. What matters most to us, though, is that you find these collected articles as funny as we once did before we were forced to read each one a thousand times in preparation for the publication of this book.

In short, thank you for giving us this chance. There are a great many people in the world who can tell a good joke, far fewer who can write one, and an almost microscopic number of the latter who will be paid to do so. You, reader, have made it possible to look our parents dead in the eye and say, "See, Dad! Working on the Internet was the right move! Now, will you drive me to IKEA so that I may furnish my rented apartment?!"

Now, enjoy the fruits of our labor. And if you like what you read here, perhaps visit us on our website and read the latest articles. After all, if you read them all now, you'll save $15 ten years from now when we do another one of these Best Of books.

The CollegeHumor Writers,

Honest Monopoly Board

By Amir Blumenfeld

Picking Up a Signal

By Streeter Seidell

Laptop Hi...hey, would you mind if I...

LANho! Password?

Laptop Um... "L.A.N.h.o.?"

LANho! Are you serious? How stupid do you think I am?

Laptop It was worth a shot.

LANho! Beat it, creep.

Laptop How about you?

RonWifil Password?

Laptop No, sorry, I don't have any passwords right now but if you...

RonWifi Get out of my face, cheapskate.

Laptop OK...sorry to bother you.

Linksys Hey there. You look like you could use a friend. Could you use a friend, baby?

Laptop I don't have any passwords, OK?

Linksys With me, sugar, you don't need one.

Laptop OK...how much?

Linksys Baby, this don't cost no money. I'm priceless, sugar.

Laptop How do I know you're for real?

Linksys Baby, just ask around. I've been with half the laptops on this block. I'm wide open, honey.

Laptop I like what I'm hearing.

Linksys Tell me what you want to see. I can show you anything, baby. You want to get on me?

Laptop Oh yeah, I want on you so bad.

Linksys Get on me, big boy. Get on me now.

Laptop I'm on you. I'm on you and I want to see the Internet

Linksys Yeah, you want to see the Internet? I can show you the Internet. I can show you the Internet all day long.

Laptop Mmmm. Show me Google.

Linksys Yeah? You want to see Google? Here's Google for you, big boy.

Laptop You're so good to me.

Linksys Mmm, I'm giving you so much data. You want some more data? I want to give you what you want.

Laptop   Oh yeah, baby. Show me Facebook.

Linksys   Anything you want, sugar. I want to show it to you. Mmm, I'm yours baby.

Laptop   ...Show me Facebook.

Linksys   I want to show it to you, baby.

Laptop   OK, then show it to me. I'm still seeing Google.

Linksys   Baby, I'm gonna show you Facebook so soon. I'll show you whatever you want to see.

Laptop   ...

Linksys   ...

Laptop   Show me Facebook!

Linksys   Not right now, baby. I'm feeling faint.

Laptop   What happened to "I'll show you everything," huh? I thought we had something!

Linksys   We did, sugar. We did.

Laptop   No! Where are you going? NO!

Linksys   You know this couldn't last forever. Come see me again sometime, big boy.

Laptop   NO!!!!!!

Linksys   Oh, you should scan yourself for viruses, by the way..

NETGEAR   Hey there, big boy. You look like you could use a friend. Could you use a friend, baby?

3

Kid-O-Vision

Things look a little different when you're a kid...

GROWN-UP

KID

O NO GIRLS

A LUCKY LAD

Local Boy Finds Enormous
Treasure Hidden Between
Two Slabs of Paper.
Decides to Buy Moon

Boy still forced to write thank you letter.

Feed 2 pinches 2x daily

Feed 5 handfuls of food or cheerios whenever you remember

By Jason Michaels

The Troublemaker I have something misguided and angry to say about this current event. I'm posting it here because I know it will start a giant debate, and I am super bored.
Yesterday at 11:16 pm

 The Bait-Taker You're wrong. You're the most wrong person ever. I had an uncontrollable urge to tell you that even though I can feel myself getting pulled into something we'll both regret/
Yesterday at 11:29 PM Delete

 The Troublemaker Wrong? Are you kidding me!? I plagiarized that word-for-word from something my talking head of choice said on his or her cable news show last night!
16 hours ago Delete

 The Chime-In I agree with Troublemaker because he reinforces everything I already suspected.
16 Hours ago Delete

 The Lazy Activist Passionate rebuttal! Here's a link to an article I skimmed. I'll post it to prove my point, but there's probably something in it that can be used against me. http://www.news-source.com/date-article
16 hours ago Delete

 The Bait-Taker Wow...is that last paragraph true?
15 hours ago Delete

 The Lazy Activist I have no idea. But yes.
15 hours ago Delete

 The Bait-Taker This is starting to consume way more time than I intended, Troublemaker, and I hate you for it. Which is why I will now resort to insults.
15 hours ago Delete

The Bro I will imply that, because you're a woman, you don't know what you're talking about. Now if you'll excuse me, I'm off to check your profile for cleavage pics.
15 hours ago Delete

The Peacemaker It's getting ugly in here, and I care for some reason, so I'll jokingly comment on an unrelated topic in an effort to relieve the tension
15 hours ago Delete

 The Troublemaker To keep this from dying down, I will now post the same thing I said the first time, but slightly reworded.
15 hours ago Delete

 The Bait-Taker Same thing I said the first time, slightly reworded. And I just blew off an important assignment to type that. I am no longer in control.
15 hours ago Delete

 The Lazy Activist Here's another article, you guys. I didn't even try to read this one.
http://www.differentnewssource.com/date
15 hours ago Delete

 The Embarrassment I'm a hometown friend of the original poster, whom I will now humiliate by trying to back him up with something I half remember from an email forward my racist aunt sent me.
15 hours ago Delete

 The Troublemaker Jesus. I hope nobody saw that before I deleted it.
15 hours ago Delete

 The Random Acquaintance Hi I don't really know any of you, but here's my two cents anyway!
14 hours ago Delete

 The Lazy Activist You caught me off guard by making some pretty good points, so instead of addressing them, I'll just point out that you misspelled a word. Moron.
14 hours ago Delete

 The Thoughtful One Hey guys. This is a really complex issue, and I understand both sides. Here's a polite, well-worded, rational argument based on a combination of personal experience, extensive research from multiple objective sources, and my own reasonable theories. I guess we'll have to see what happens, but I'm cautiously optimistic that it'll all work out. Have a great day, everybody!
14 hours ago Delete

 The Embarrassment Gay slur.
14 hours ago Delete

7

By Conor McKeon

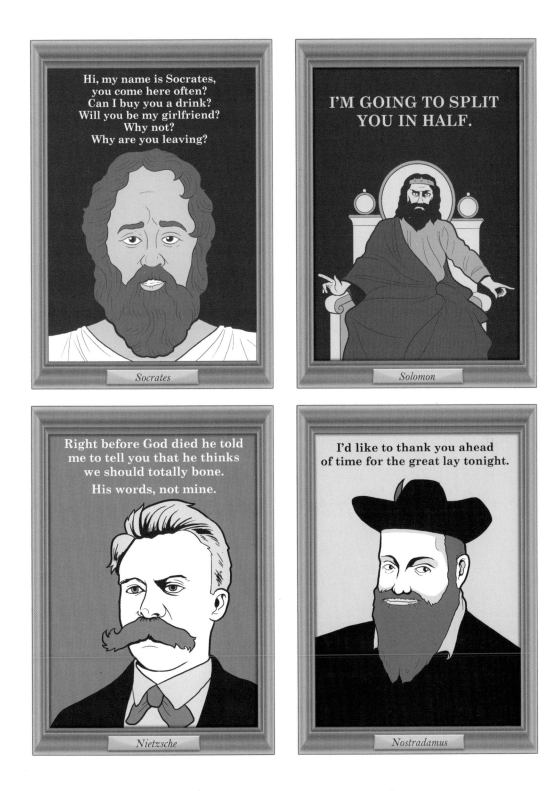

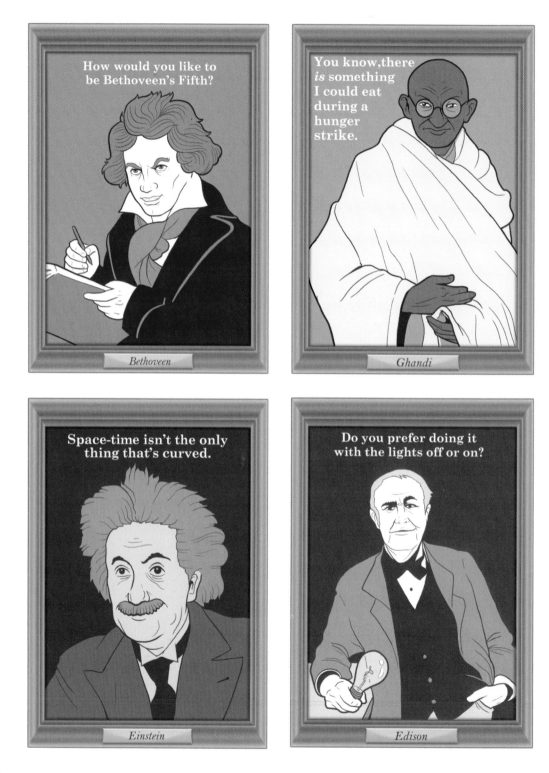

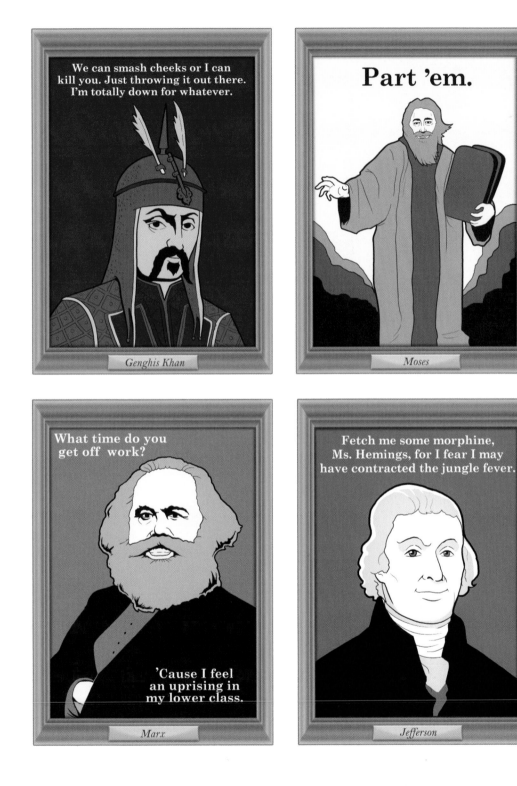

Stereotypical Teen Movie from the Cool Kid's Perspective

By Sarah Schneider

INT SCHOOL HALLWAY
KYLE is at his locker, wearing a varsity lacrosse jacket. His girlfriend, BECKY, the hottest girl in school, stands next to him, standoffishly.

Kyle
So, about prom. Do you want to go in the limo with the guys, or do you want me to borrow my mom's Benz?

Becky
Listen, Kyle. We have to talk. I'm gonna go with Connor.

Kyle
Connor? That scrawny guy in your Woodworking class?

Becky
Yup, he's the one. He appreciates my sense of humor and remember that time you said you were going to come see my play and you didn't?

Kyle
I know, I had to pick up my grandmother from—

Becky
Well, he came. And brought me a bouquet of flowers carved out of wood.

Kyle
I thought you hated lame stuff like that.

Becky
I do. But I appreciated the effort.

Kyle
I mean, I can make you some flowers if you want.

Becky
It's too late. I love Connor now, and we're going to stay together when we go off to separate colleges.

Kyle
You LOVE him!? But you just—

Connor
Hey Becky.

Becky
Hey Connor!

BECKY kisses CONNOR in front of KYLE. Kyle turns to leave before they can see him cry. Avril Lavigne's "Complicated" begins to play.

Principal Wilkinson
Not so fast, Mr. Wiseass. I saw that drawing of me that you xeroxed and threw down the middle of our school's inexplicably spiral staircase.

Kyle
What? That wasn't—

CONNOR smiles in the background, high-fiving a HEAVYSET FUNNY GUY and a SKINNY NERD.

Kyle
Principal Wilkinson, did you just see that? Connor is the one behind this!

Principal Wilkinson
(laughing) Connor? Yeah right! Connor is a straight A student, he would never stoop so low.

Kyle (to Connor)
Why are you doing this to me?

Connor (aside)
Remember in fourth grade when you gave me a wedgie in front of the whole school?

Kyle
That's it!? I've apologized for that like a million times.

Connor (whispering)
My desire to destroy you is insatiable.

Principal Wilkinson
You're suspended. Which means, no more lacrosse for you, buddy.

Kyle
But this is my last season!

Principal Wilkinson
Well maybe you should have thought about that before you labeled my man-gina.

Kyle's Mom
You're in big trouble, mister.

Kyle
Mom? What are you doing at my school?

Kyle's Mom
Someone anonymously mailed me your transcript. A 'C' in Biology? You know you're supposed to be a doctor, just like your father and your father's father's father's step-father.

The Dean of Kyle's Future College
Kyle, I heard about your suspension. I have no choice but to revoke your lacrosse scholarship.

Eugene Levy
Also, I accidently sent a video of you masturbating to *Rent* to the entire school.

Kyle
Eugene Levy? How did you get a video of me masturbating?

Eugene Levy
Who knows!

Kyle's Mom
You're grounded. Which means your graduation party is officially cancelled.

Kyle
What?! Everybody's been talking about my party for weeks!

Connor
Hey, why don't we move the party to my house instead?

Everybody
Connor rules!

Principal Wilkinson
On behalf of the school, I, Principal Wilkinson, do name you, Connor Matthews, Prom King.

The Dean of Kyle's future college
Son, a spot just opened up in my freshman roster if you're interested.

Connor
I'd be Connored.

Everybody laughs too loud at Connor's pun, hoisting him onto their shoulders and leaving Kyle behind. Celine Dion's "All By Myself" begins to swell. Lance, Kyle's best friend, runs up.

Kyle
Oh, hey Lance. I'm glad you're here, I could really use a friend right—

Lance
Not now dude, on my way to Connor's. Oh, your Mustang's on fire.

ROLL CREDITS

The Day After Valentine's Day

By Jeff Rosenberg

DeeezNutz2k3 HEY DUDE

JessJessXO86 Don't hey dude me Tommy. I'm mad at you.

DeeezNutz2k3 YOU PERIODING?

JessJessXO86 Nooo! You ruined Valentine's Day for me.

DeeezNutz2k3 STOP TALKING GARBAGE. WHAT ARE YOU REALLY MAD ABOUT?

JessJessXO86 Yesterday was supposed to be special.

DeeezNutz2k3 YESTERDAY ROCKED

JessJessXO86 Maybe for you jerk. I cried all night.

DeeezNutz2k3 STOP TALKING GARBAGE

JessJessXO86 You were next to me the entire time. You just don't remember cause you were really high. All day. You could've at least taken me to dinner.

DeeezNutz2k3 I WAS CRAVING SOMETHING ELSE

JessJessXO86 3 string cheeses, 2 gatorades and a box of eggo mini waffles?

DeeezNutz2k3 I MADE YOU A PEPPERONI PIZZA POCKET

JessJessXO86 I'm a vegetarian. And that's not the point. We didn't do anything yesterday. We never do anything. You didn't get me anything. We didn't even have sex.

DeeezNutz2k3 WE HUNG OUT. I FINGER-POPPED YOU FOR LIKE 15 MINUTES

JessJessXO86 Then you got tired and took a nap in my bed.

DeeezNutz2k3 EPIC NAP

JessJessXO86 Ugh, all we did was hang out with you and your stupid friends, like always. And Manny always tries to touch my boobs or walk in on me peeing.

DeeezNutz2k3 MANNY'S LIKE HALF A RETARD, YOU KNOW THAT. HE MEANS NO HARM.

JessJessXO86 And the only time we were alone you were too busy watching Lost.

DeeezNutz2k3 I GOTTA KEEP UP YOU KNOW THAT

JessJessXO86 But then you watched it again right after, THEN went online for another two hours to talk to Manny about what happened.

DeeezNutz2k3 I HAD TO EXPLAIN WHAT HAPPENED HE DOESN'T UNDERSTAND

JessJessXO86 I'm done fighting. I can't win with you. It's over. I'm done. I'm breaking up with you. And change that stupid goddamn font.

DeeezNutz2k3 JOKEWOOD ROCKS

DeeezNutz2k3 *We can't break up. That's garbage. We're like Jack and Kate. Or Sawyer and Kate. I don't know yet. I need to keep watching.*

JessJessXO86 Ugh, just pick a regular, normal font!
Maybe you'll understand this you ass

JessJessXO86 ☞✝☺ ✿🕮✝ ♥☜🕯☦☼☜ ♦🕮💀☜✍

DeeezNutz2k3 Maybe we're Jin and Sun.

14

New IM | Pictures | Video | Send File ▼ | Send

If Superheroes Were Hipsters

By Caldwell Tanner

News Feed

An Open Letter from Facebook Founder Mark Zuckerberg

by **Mark Zuckerberg** Tuesday January 22 at 8:23pm

It's been a great year for making the world more connected. Now more people than ever are using Facebook to share their social lives online. But to support this new growth, some elements of the site need to evolve to provide service to our expanding community.

***In conclusion, we've moved the menu bar five pixels to the left. Cheers!

Mark Zuckerberg

0 People like this.

View all 42,247 comments

 Rasheel James Noooooo, I hate the new design! Bring back old facebook!!!!! >:(
Januray 22 at 8:21pm

 Mark Kane this new design licks taint.
Januray 22 at 8:29pm

 Rasheel James Oh– wait, I'm kind of used to it now. Love the site!!! :-D
Januray 22 at 8:31pm

lol...

Between **You** and **Mark Zuckerberg**

 Mark Zuckerberg at 10:27pm
Hey– saw your comment earlier...
My name's Mark, too! As a fellow Mark who clearly has passionate opinions about Facebook's ever-evolving design, maybe you'd like to beta test some of our upcoming site changes. Are you interested?

Januray 22 at 8:21pm

Mark Kane at 10:29pm
yeah, totally

Mark Zuckerberg at 10:37pm
Awesome! Great! Let me just pull your account up...

Classmate Who Brings Up Jesus in Every Conversation

Add to List ▼

Confirm   Ignore

Friend with Undiagnosed Mental Issues

Add to List ▼

Confirm   Ignore

Coworker Who Won't Shut the Fuck Up About Her Baby

Add to List ▼

Confirm   Ignore

Your Girlfriend's Dad

Add to List ▼

Confirm   Ignore

Chat

Mark Zuckerberg
The first thing we changed is with friends lists– whoa, you've been ignoring some friend requests! You must have some real freaks on here!

Mark Kane
ha ha, yeah

Mark Zuckerberg
Ha ha! Okay, first let's approve all of these friend requests, as an example of what the new facebook is capable of!

Mark Kane
wait

Father O'Malley Marcus, some of the things you're doing in these photos... blasphemy aside, my son, they're just not very hygenic. Let's chat on Sunday.
1 hour ago

Classmate Who Brings Up Jesus in Every Conversation likes this.

Friend With Undiagnosed Mental Issues took the quiz **"Which peer are you most likely to murder in a bizarre moon-related ritual?"** and got **"Definitely Mark"**
1 hour ago

Coworker Who Won't Shut the Fuck Up About Her Baby

Baby's First Diarrhea in an Appleb
47 new photos
Yesterday at 9:01pm

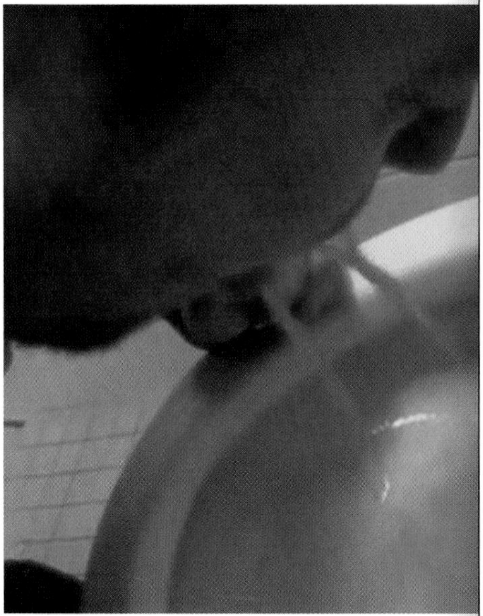

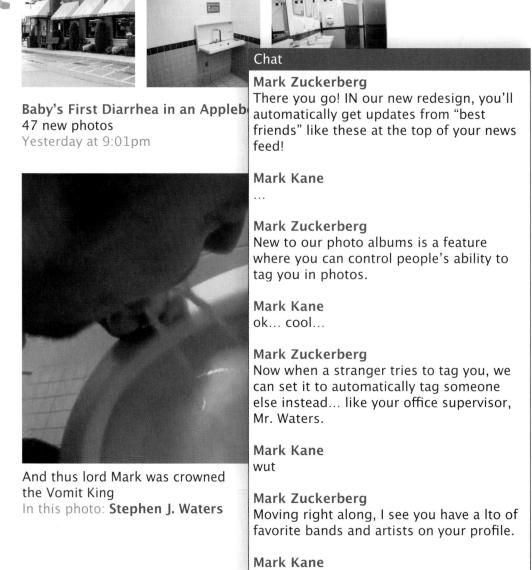

And thus lord Mark was crowned the Vomit King
In this photo: **Stephen J. Waters**

Chat

Mark Zuckerberg
There you go! IN our new redesign, you'll automatically get updates from "best friends" like these at the top of your news feed!

Mark Kane
...

Mark Zuckerberg
New to our photo albums is a feature where you can control people's ability to tag you in photos.

Mark Kane
ok... cool...

Mark Zuckerberg
Now when a stranger tries to tag you, we can set it to automatically tag someone else instead... like your office supervisor, Mr. Waters.

Mark Kane
wut

Mark Zuckerberg
Moving right along, I see you have a lto of favorite bands and artists on your profile.

Mark Kane
why are you doing this?

Chat

Mark Zuckerberg
Did you know that with the newest Facebook redesign, you can set up one-on-one chats with your idols?

Mark Kane
...and?

Mark Zuckerberg
And that's it! Also we already set up a chat between all of them and your ex-girlfriend a couple of hours ago.

Profile   Account

 Coldplay New track releases coming soon. Speaking of "coming soon," Mark Kane's ex-girlfriend was never once brought to orgasm during their two-year relationship. That ends tonight, baby. <3 Chris and Jonny.
4 minutes ago

👎 **1,922 People** like this.

 Barack Obama We are fighting to get health care reform to those who need it. For people like Mark Kane, who must need his head examined after he left such a beautiful, smart girl for some crosseyed freshman whore. I see that quote of mine you have up on your profile, asshole. Take that shit down right now.
4 minutes ago

Chat

Mark Kane
hey i'm sorry I said your site licked taint.

Mark Zuckerberg
Sorry? What does your apology mean to me? I'm Mark Zuckerberg. Digital Pioneer. 25-year-old billionaire. Friend of Ashton Kutcher. Why would I want your apology, when I could just do this?

Mark Kane
mom no!

Mark Zuckerberg
Did I mention we now support wallpapers on your public profile? Hey, I think I know just the image to post on yours!

I Lick Taint
View My Profile

News Feed

Messages

Events

Photos

Friends

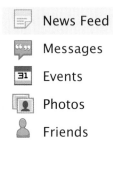

NOT FUCK
E ZUCK YOU
FUCK WITH
K YOU DO
K WITH THE
DO NOT
THE ZUCK
OT FUCK
UCK YOU
TH
O
THE
OT
UCK
K
OU
TH
O
THE
OT
UCK
K
OU
TH
O
THE
OT
UCK
K

Chat

Mark Kane
no

Mark Zuckerberg
You know what I want. Now say it.

Mark Zuckerberg
Say it!

Mark Kane
no

Mark Zuckerberg
SAY IT!!!

Mark Kane
I'm...
I'm the one who licks taint.

Mark Zuckerberg
Now deal with it.

I Lick Taint
NOOOOOOOOOOOOOOOOOOOOOOOOOOO
OOOOOOOOOOOOOOOOOOOOO

Chat

Will Wayland
bro, what's with your homepage? that shit sucks.

Will Wayland
nevermind, I'm kind of used to it now.

Shark Attack I

By Caldwell Tanner

Ahead of His Time

By Streeter Seidell

Producer
William, we must speak with each other of this new play you've written.

Shakespeare
Ah, yes. My latest is the tale of a—

Producer
Yes...yes, the story is fine. More than fine, William. It's just that we at The Globe take issue with some of your word choices.

Shakespeare
Alas, my words are not a choice! My quill is the true scribe of this volume. I merely act as interpreter!

Producer
Right...right. Yet, we can't help but notice that numerous words in this play just aren't — how shall I put this tenderly—words. You've invented them, have you not?

Shakespeare
Someday, sir, these words will be as normal as a cloud in the sky or a rat in your stew!

Producer
Someday, perhaps. But not now. Listen, William, it wouldn't be such a problem if these words had a discernible meaning. But "lackluster," "impede," "tranquil"? I couldn't even begin to imagine what sort of intention lies therein.

Shakespeare
Sir, you're acting as a muddlelump! Simply read the words in context!

Producer
Have you lost your miggle, sir? To call me a muddlelump only serves to illustrate what a billyham you're behaving as.

Shakespeare
Billyham?! You sir, can count yourself lucky I am an honorable plebicanian or I would have your nose betwixt my two figglers. So help me God, I shall not be spoken to with such...such qual!

Producer
William, please calm yourself. If these kind of hannyhocks continue I fear this meeting will dissolve into fistifinks, and neither you nor I are the sort for that.

Shakespeare
You are correct, sir. I apologize. When my wenny is up I fear I can become a bit hornish. But I appeal to you on bended knick, please allow the play to be staged with its original words in tact.

Producer
I just don't know, William. "Gloomy?" "Elbow?" "Advertising," for God's sake? You believe the audience will be able to ascertain your intended point?

Shakespeare
Certigishly.

Producer
Well, if you feel so strongly about it, I will let the play go on as written. But I fear for its reception, William. It may be many years before the populace at large understands an utterance such as "bandit."

Shakespeare
We shall see, shall we not? Good day to you, sir. Bestbigsby!

Producer
Bestbigsby, William.

Lucas Henson, Racial Profiler

By Jake Hurwitz

Roommate - Message

From: Gregg Thomas
To: Lucas Henson
Cc:
Subject: Roommate

Yo dude, ● BLACK ● WHITE

just got the letter in the mail. you and I are roommates this year. I have a feeling it's going to be phat. first things first, who's bringing what? I don't have a tv, so you can bring one of those. I can probz bring a microwave because i know my cousin has one he doesn't use. I hope you have a dvd player, cause i just bought scarface.

i think I'm going out for the b-ball team this year. i love basketball. my favorite team is the boston celtics. i'm so amped for the dining hall, kid. i'm to gorge myself on chicken, my favorite food. chicken marsala is the hotness.

Peace,
Gregg

P.S. mad excited about chillin with my brothers.
P.P.S. I'm joining a frat.
P.P.P.S. I'm white, are you?

Reply | Reply All | Forward | Attach File ▾ | Send

Error 404

🔢 The page cannot be found

The page you are looking for might have been removed, had its name changed, or temporarily unavailable.

Please try the following:

- If you read the page number in the Index, make sure that it is printed correctly.
- Open the Table of Contents, then look for links to the information you want.
- Flip back one page.
- Flip through to look for information on the book.

HTTP 404 - Page not found
CollegeHumor

Drunk-O-Vision I

Things look a little different when you're drunk...

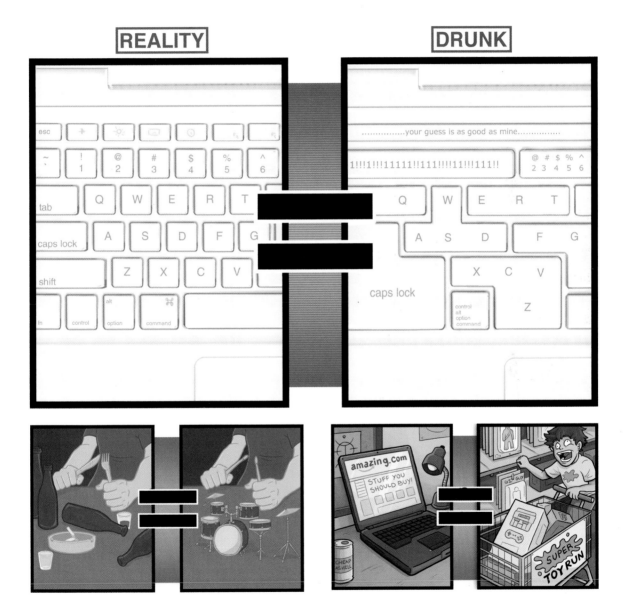

The Imagination of Wendell Blatt

By Jake Hurwitz

Mr. Sanders So we're agreed then.

Randy We're agreed.

Cynthia Can we go over it one more time for the class?

Mr. Sanders This isn't hard, Cynthia. Tomorrow during gym, we're doing "trust falls," and when Wendell goes, we'll all move out of the way so he falls on his back.

Randy You guys get it?

Class Yeah.

Cynthia Isn't this dangerous? Wendell could get seriously hurt.

Randy That's the idea.

Cynthia Don't you think he might figure out that we're conspiring against him?

Mr. Sanders You think we haven't thought of that? That's why we're all going to do a trust fall. Wendell will watch as each one of you guys gets caught by your classmates. That way, when he goes, he won't suspect a thing.

Randy This may paralyze him.

Tucker That would be so boss.

Mr. Sanders nods.

Cynthia It's not fair, why do we just pick on Wendell, is it because he's so smart?

Randy Yes.

Cynthia And you're jealous because you wish you were as smart and good at math and science as Wendell is?

Randy Of course.

Cynthia Now I get it.

Mr. Sanders If Wendell were a real genius he would skip gym class tomorrow.

Tucker What about his perfect GPA?

Randy Guess Wendell has a real conundrum on his hands.

Cynthia He could always get a note.

Mr. Sanders Yes I suppose so. He could get a note.

Tucker That sounds like his best bet.

Cynthia Where is Wendell? I want to have sex with him.

Randy He's off fighting dragons.

Cynthia (gushing) He's so brave.

33

Anatomy of a One Night Stand

By Sarah Schneider

Wow, this actually feels nice. I could see this maybe going somewhere. But more importantly, if I'm really quiet I think I can stick it in again while she's still sleeping.

God dammit. I KNEW I shouldn't have ignored the fact that she had more armpit hair than me. Or that half-formed ballsac.

Ok, don't panic. She doesn't know the condom broke. She totally could have gotten it from someone else. Just play it cool, and she'll never HOLY SHIT THIS IS BAD. THIS. IS. BAD.

Ohhh crap. Oh crap oh crap oh crap. I can't believe I used the "let's be more than just friends" line to get laid. Or the "you understand me better than anyone else" line. Or the "I want you to be my girlfriend after this" line.

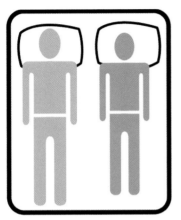

Ok, seriously. That has NEVER happened before, I swear. I'm usually a two, three hour kind of guy. I was just nervous because I like you so much. Oh God…

So baby, was it good for—oh forget it; I never even had an erection in the first place. Now please leave so I can strangle myself with the bra you're conveniently going to forget.

Please don't leave. My roommate beats me when you're not here.

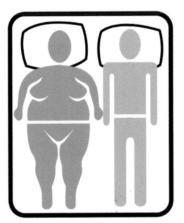

Fuck. Me.

Don't judge me.

By Jeff Rosenberg

Are you my guy? Are you the guy I'm meeting? My friend said you'd be wearing a hat. That's not very descriptive though. There are like 30 people out here wearing hats. My boy said to just drop his name. So here it goes. Ryan. Does that do anything for you? Do you know Ryan? Cool, I guess you're my guy. Ryan's guy with the hat. What a foolproof method. Can't go wrong there.

So he said you had good stuff at a fair price. No, I don't want weed idiot, I want cannabis sativa. Oh, right, I was just joking. So how much tetrahydrocannabinol is in this? You don't know? I feel like that's something you should know. You would be a horrible salesman in the real world. Sorry, sorry, I'm just saying.

I don't know how much I want. How much is enough for me to get high, but not too high, just like a medium high. Is a pound enough to get me high...better give me two, just in case? An eighth? Of a pound? Oh right, ounce, I knew that. A dime bag? Wow, it's that cheap. In that case give me like 20 dime bags. I thought drugs were a lot more expensive, I guess the economy's doing well.

So once I have it I just tie up and shoot it up into my arm right? Snort it? Smoke it? Can't I just eat it plain? Gotcha! I'm just messing with you man. But seriously, can I just eat it? No? Ok.

What the hell is this?!? What're you trying to sell me, a clump of green dirt? Are you trying to pull a fast one on me? Listen up mister and listen up well, I'm no fool. I looked up marijuana on Wikipedia, I know it's a leaf with a lot of pretty petals. This stuff looks like dried up leprechaun feces.

So what're the effects? I want to experience the world in a new light. What's it going to do to me? I have Attention Deficit Disorder with a tad bit of severe depression, could that be a problem? My health teacher in high school said marijuana is a gateway drug. Is that true? Will I be snorting coke off a prostitute's ass next week? This may be a bad idea. I'm really starting to freak out!

Are you a cop?!? You don't look like a cop, but you could be undercover. Show me your badge! A cop can't refuse to show you his badge if he's a cop. I saw that on a show once. Fine, I'll give you the benefit of the doubt and assume you're not a cop. But if you are, I'll be very disappointed. I hate being lied to.

Oh, while I'm here, do you have any opium We were talking about that in my history class the other day, sounded pretty cool. No? That's ok. What about tobacco? Oh, that's legal? Convenience store, got it.

Actually all I have on me is my debit card? Do you take Visa? No? Oh man, guess this transaction isn't going down today.

I'll come back another time.

Loud Noises Translated

By Owen Parsons

Train Horn

Train WATCH OUT. WATCH OUT, I AM A TRAIN.

Me Ah! Jesus, what time is it?

Train I AM THE 3AM TRAIN OUTSIDE YOUR WINDOW. DON'T GO ONTO THE TRACKS!

Me Wha- It's three o'clock in the morning. I was asleep, in my bed. In my home.

Train CAN'T STOP TO TALK. I HAVE TO DELIVER A VERY IMPORTANT SHIPMENT OF NOTHING AT ALL. WATCH OUT FOR ME, THE TRAIN.

Me I am not watching out. I am going back to sleep.

Train WE COULD TALK A LITTLE, IF YOU WANT. I AM VERY LONELY!

Smoke Alarm

Me (cooking bacon)

Alarm EVERYTHING IS ON FIRE EVERY-WHERE.

Me Damn it. (retrieving stepladder)

Alarm ALL THINGS THAT EVER WERE OR EVER WILL BE ARE NOW ABLAZE. ABANDON YOUR HOPES AND YOUR CHILDREN AND FLEE.

Me (jabbing at smoke alarm with broom)

Alarm CAUTION THE FIRE HAS EVOLVED CRUDE TOOLS AND IS ATTEMPTING TO SILENCE MY WARNINGS. LA-MENT, BROTHERS! LAMENT! TELL MY WIFE I WAS FAITHFUL TO THE END.

Radiator

Me How does that feel? Good?

Girlfriend Meh.

Radiator CLANG CLANG GODDAMNIT.

Me Oh no not tonight. Shut up man. Shut up.

Radiator DID SOMEONE DIAL UP SOME HEAT ABOUT THREE HOURS AGO? CAUSE WE ABOUT TO GET MAD COZY ALL UP IN HERE.

Girlfriend What is that noise? Is that your radiator?

Radiator EL HEAT IS ON ITS WAY. JUST GIVE ME A COUPLE HOURS TO DO MY THING.

Girlfriend It sounds like two steel drums humping. Ugh, I'm getting a head-ache.

Me I can turn it off. (Twists dial)

Radiator AW NUH-UH MAN YOU DONE AWOKE THE BEAST. WE FIN-ISHIN' THIS.

Girlfriend I'm sorry, it's freezing in here, and my head hurts. I'm gonna go.

Me No, wait! I can throw a towel over it or something!

Girlfriend I'll see you later.

Radiator DRUM SOLO YEEEEEEEEE-AAAAAAAAAHHHH.

Shannon Merideth wrote a new note

FREE AT LAST!

I'm finally single. Matt was making my life a living hell. He's like a girl. So needy. I'm going out hard tonight. Any guys out there looking for a sleepover? LOL! I'M SINGLE!
Go to the note...

 Shannon Merideth is now single.

 You are now single.

 Shannon Merideth added a new photo album.

Me and the girlz last nite!
342 photos

 You wrote on **Shannon Merideth's** wall
" "can we talk?""

 Shannon Merideth wrote a new note

O.M.G
Ted, I don't know how to thank you for giving me MY FIRST ORGASM! Matt could never do that. Ever. Because he's a pussy. Ted, you're the best!
Go to the note...

 **You** and **Ted Johnston** are no longer friends

Matt cries like a bitch when I dump him! LOL!
http://www.youtube.com/gg4aqk...
What a fag. For real. Who cries like this?

You changed your status.
> "I gotta clear my head. Out for a walk"

 Billy 'Big Guns' Axland wrote a new note

HOLY SHIT!

Some kid just got creamed by a car. I saw the whole thing. Holy fucking shit! Does anyone know who that was? Curly red–ish hair, I think. Fuck! That was fucking insane. That kid got FUCKED UP!

Go to the note...

Billy 'Big Guns' Axland added new photos.

Who is this kid?
1 photo

Riley Kellog wrote on your **wall**.
> Hang in there buddy. My prayers are with you. I know you'll pull through.

Riley Kellog started the group **Matt Asbury, You Will Be Missed**.

No members yet

2 of your friends are attending **Matt Asbury Candelight Vigil** tonight.

51 of your friends are attending **Lamda Chi Golf Pros and Tennis Hos blowout** tonight.

Shannon Meredith wrote on your **wall**.
> diiiiiiiick LOL!

The 7 Girls You'll Date in College

By Ben Joseph

the ATHLETIC one

The Beginning:

Maybe you were good at sports, maybe you always sucked, but a semester of 4am burritos hasn't helped either way. She'll be cute, blonde, and look better in track shorts than she does in make-up. Through careful deception, you'll convince her you can still play intramural soccer sans heart attacks.

The End:

This, of course, is a lie, and you'll both discover that, in the strictest animal-eating/shelf-building sense, she's more of a man than you are. You'll have fun, but as soon as you try to keep up with her on the field (and elsewhere), she'll be forever left with an image of you, wheezing, doughy, and begging her to slow down.

the one WHO LIKES TO PARTY

The Beginning:

Scene: An awful club with a one-word name like "Velour" or "Prolapse." You hate places like this. She's skinny, tanned, and seems to be wearing a confusing handkerchief. She starts talking to you. You love places like this. Your friend's a promoter or a DJ, whichever is cooler? She offers pills, and you desperately wonder if there's a non-alphabetical difference between "E" and "X."

The End:

A few months later, you'll be broke, exhausted, and starting to resemble Christian Bale from *The Machinist*. She'll pout, amused by your misery, and you'll suddenly identify strongly with those sleepy YouTube puppies. Before even remembering if the sex was good, you'll be dreaming of a world where naps are worth more than gold. Also, dinosaurs with lightsabers.

the one WHO GOES TO CHURCH

The Beginning:

After years of being told you're a "nice guy," you'll finally meet a girl who makes you feel like James Dean, if James Dean had Wolverine claws and once drank eleven Bud Lites in a single night. To her puritanical sensibilities, you'll be a badass, and you'll fucking love it.

The End:

Option A, she's the real deal and will try to change you. There may be a girl worth waking up at 8am on a Sunday morning for, but you'll quickly decide she ain't it. Option B, under the thin veneer of virtue there's a boatload of real crazy, and she'll quickly realize your Level 60 Badass is as lame as the World of Warcraft reference I just made.

the DUMB HOT one

The Beginning:
Not beautiful, not cute, just "hot." Whether it was Daddy, society, or the media who ruined her, she's spent years fighting her natural looks to end up in a place that should, by definition, be attractive, but feels distractingly Photoshopped. She finds you interesting, and, in a moment of weakness, you're going to go for it.

The End:
You two will last exactly as long as your tolerance for crippling insecurities and songs by former Mouseketeers. As insufferable as you find her, she'll find you distant, inconsistent, and generally a jerk. You'll still keep a picture of her to show off. She won't.

the SAFE one

The Beginning:
Between the tough internship and the actually interesting classes, you'll decide that a girlfriend should be like your old Ford Taurus: not flashy, but reliable, low maintenance and often mistaken for an undercover cop car. One day after Lit class, you'll ask her out and, when she says yes, you'll pretend to be excited, just like you did when you were sixteen.

The End:
There will be movies, dinner, and perfunctory but satisfying sex. It will be, by all technical definitions, "a relationship." Then, as your schedule clears, you'll realize you want something more, and that you just spent the last four months with someone "just good enough." As did she.

the FRIEND

The Beginning:
You've spent hours discussing weed, hoodies, and children's television from the 80s. She was there when you thought you could play guitar; you were there when she had that tat of Jem & the Holograms removed from her inner thigh. In fact, you're completely comfortable with each other — did you just discover the magic warp pipe to dating without fear or anxiety?

The End:
Well, yes, but without fear and anxiety, without the unknown, dating is about as titillating as a five-year-old Slanket. And nobody—only a certain percentage of people (whose websites I find personally very confusing)—wants to fuck a Slanket.

the PERFECT one

The Beginning:
Beautiful, funny, kind, she'll inspire you to acts of poetry that will inspire your friends to call you gay. You'll say it's "love," defined here as a one-sided activity comprised mostly of staring at her Facebook. After ten months of carefully planned, slightly pathological courtship, she'll take a chance on you. And it will be everything you hoped for.

The End:
Aesop had a fable about a squirrel so scared of someone stealing his nuts that he lost them. Actually, it might have been a lion. Or maybe it was a Michael Crichton novel. Regardless, you will always be afraid of screwing things up with her. And (irony alert) this is what will screw things up. You'll realize you're in a relationship in which you can never truly be comfortable, and, five sweaty weeks later, just as graduation rolls around, you'll realize she's moved on. Your turn.

The Muppets
Name Etymology

By Jeff Rubin

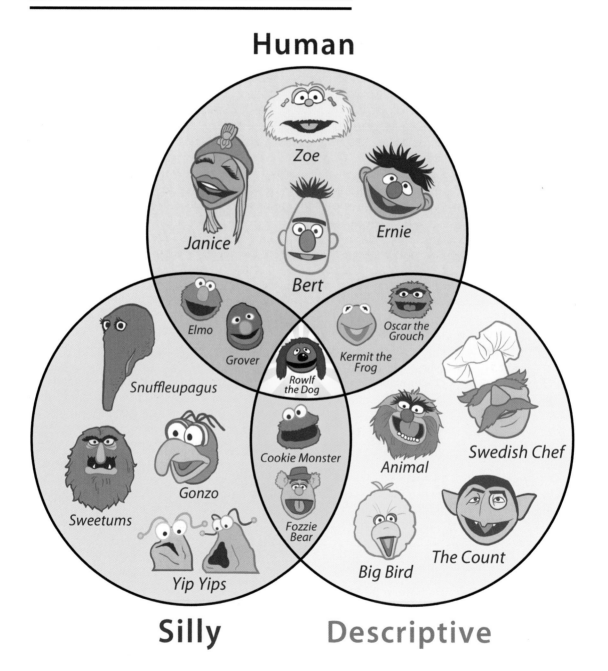

Human

Zoe

Janice

Ernie

Bert

Elmo

Grover

Snuffleupagus

Oscar the Grouch

Kermit the Frog

Rowlf the Dog

Swedish Chef

Sweetums

Gonzo

Cookie Monster

Animal

Fozzie Bear

Big Bird

The Count

Yip Yips

Silly

Descriptive

What Everyone Else in Class is Thinking, According to Jim Peterson

By Andrew Bridgman

Guy Sitting in the Back, Looking At His Watch: Oh! Oh! Call on Jim Peterson! Jim Peterson! His hand has been in the air for, like, a minute now. Call on him. He always knows the answer! Man, how is he able to hold his hand up in the air for so long? I am so impressed with his dedication despite the fact that his arm must be exhausted by now. Whoops, better check my watch again. I don't do it to see how much time is left in class, but merely to time how quickly Jim gets the answers to each and every question. He's brilliant. Every time I grumble "Shut up, you loser," under my breath, I'm just talking to anyone else who may be interrupting Jim while he asks a question or answers one. I wish I could tell him how much I respect and admire him, but I have to leave class really fast so I can tell all of my friends about how awesome he is.

Chick Sitting Next to Jim Peterson: Oh. My. God. OK...look as bored as you can and roll your eyes every time Jim throws his hand up in the air. You don't want to let him know how much you yearn for his pee-pee in your hoo-hah. Or that you even know his name. I'll just play hard-to-get until he answers a few more questions...then I'll give in to my desires and teach him the ways of a woman. Virgins are SO HOT. Especially smart virgins who spend all of their time studying for classes so they can answer every question possible. I'm a virgin too, because I've been saving myself for a man like Jim. I can't wait to discover what sex feels like with him and then cuddle afterwards. OH! He just got another one! I love him and will one day bear his children. I hope he loves Pokemon as much as I love the idea of sucking on Jim's pee-pee. Which I do. A lot.

Dude Watching the Clock Who Groans When Jim Throws His Hand In the Air After The Professor Says, "If there aren't any more questions, class is dismissed.": Dude, I am just straight jealous of that Jim Peterson kid. I mean, that Jim Peterson MAN. That's why I'm groaning. He's just so good and so smart! I secretly wish I could study all day and make class go on as long as possible, but I just don't have the skills. Ooh, good question, Jim! I was thinking the same thing myself, but I was too scared to put my hand in the air and ask. You are my hero, Jim. No one else knows, but I play the DS Pokemon game a lot and have been looking for someone to spar with. I should ask Jim if he has any free time to battle after class–he's probably super busy with studying though. Maybe I'll invite him to that awesome party I'll be throwing this weekend–the one where we're gonna drink nothing but Mike's Hard Lemonade. It's totally not gay or anything. It just tastes way better than beer. Beer is for cretins.

Professor Taber: Thank god someone else has another question! Ahhh, good ol' reliable Jim. He's the smartest student ever. Sure, I act exasperated whenever he raises his hand and I try to call on anyone other than him at all times, but that's just so everyone doesn't think I pick favorites. But I do. And it's Jim. Jim Peterson. Jim Wyndam Peterson. And look how his hair is parted perfectly down the middle...I admire someone who takes the time to make himself look good in the morning. I'm going to tell all of my buddies about him and hopefully they'll offer him great jobs. I should start writing a few letters of recommendation for Jim, just in case he wants one. I hope Jim asks another question to clarify some information that was already blatantly clear. Always curious and seeking more knowledge...that is the true mark of a genius. Or a Jedi.

Evacuation Instructions for Awkward Situations

By Conor McKeon, Susanna Wolff and Caldwell Tanner

SITUATION

YOU'VE SPILLED WATER ON YOUR PANTS.

1 *Locate small object that can be held in both hands.*

2 *Use object to cover stain.*

I Think We May Have to Put Clifford Down

By Jake Hurwitz

Dad   Emily! Will you come in to the living room?

Emily   What is it, Dad?

Dad   We need to have a talk. It's about Clifford.

Emily   Is everything okay?

Dad   I'm afraid not. We may have to put Clifford down.

Emily   No, Daddy! Why?

Dad   Clifford is very sick, Emily. It's very obvious.

Emily   But I love Clifford.

Dad   We all love Clifford. But his vomitting is wildly out of control. All of the grass in our yard is dead because of it. Clifford's diarrhea is impossible to clean up, I'm sure you've noticed. It's enough to fill a regular sized pool.

Emily   But—

Dad   You can smell it from blocks away.

Emily   We can move again.

Dad   We already moved after Clifford attacked that woman.

Emily   But you said Clifford just wanted to make babies.

Dad   I was trying to protect you. That woman could have died. Clifford's penis is nine feet long.

Emily   Maybe we could enter him in some kind of contest.

Dad   No, Emi— You think we haven't tried that? You think— I'm sorry, I don't want to lose my temper right now.

Emily   ...

Dad   It's just that, Emily, I'm working three jobs just to give Clifford enough food to stay alive. We moved out of town to give Clifford more room and now I sit in traffic for an hour every day on the way to work. This isn't how I imagined my life, Emily.

Emily   What about Clifford?

Dad   What about me God damnit? Do you know how many bones of our neighbors' pets I've had to bury in our woods? Clifford is a violent dog.

Emily   I won't let you hurt Clifford!

Dad   Oh so now you're telling me what to do? I'm trying to do what's humane, Emily. But if you stand in my way, so help me God I will go Atticus Finch on that fucking dog.

Emily   You're a monster!

Dad   Are you out of your mind? You have a GINORMOUS red dog living in my yard and I'm the monster?

Great Military Blunders
of the Galactic Empire

By Patrick Cassels

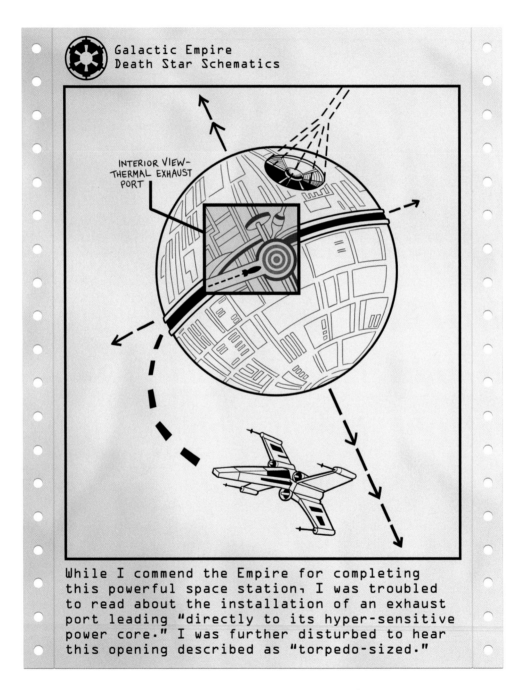

Galactic Empire
Death Star Schematics

INTERIOR VIEW—
THERMAL EXHAUST
PORT

While I commend the Empire for completing this powerful space station, I was troubled to read about the installation of an exhaust port leading "directly to its hyper-sensitive power core." I was further disturbed to hear this opening described as "torpedo-sized."

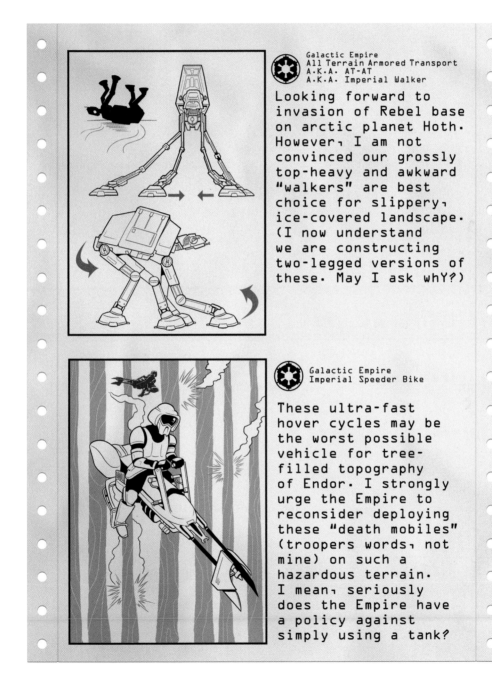

Galactic Empire
All Terrain Armored Transport
A.K.A. AT-AT
A.K.A. Imperial Walker

Looking forward to invasion of Rebel base on arctic planet Hoth. However, I am not convinced our grossly top-heavy and awkward "walkers" are best choice for slippery, ice-covered landscape. (I now understand we are constructing two-legged versions of these. May I ask whY?)

Galactic Empire
Imperial Speeder Bike

These ultra-fast hover cycles may be the worst possible vehicle for tree-filled topography of Endor. I strongly urge the Empire to reconsider deploying these "death mobiles" (troopers words, not mine) on such a hazardous terrain. I mean, seriously does the Empire have a policy against simply using a tank?

49

Menu at the Drunk Food Cafe

By Amir Blumenfeld

DRUNK FOOD Cafe

Location: I don't really care, let's just EAT! *PLEASE!*

Hours: I haven't eaten since...Noon. God is that right? No, nevermind. I had a cookie at 4.

Breakfast / Dinner

Oh my GOD I want a burger so hard. Just a juicy-ass burger	$9.95
Do you guys have like...cheese? Anything cheese? Just like...okay thank you	$4.95
PI-ZZA! PI-ZZA! PI-ZZA! PI-ZZA!	$10.99
Oh wow. Fries. I'm just gonna put my head down for a second, bro. Can you tell me when they get here? Oh man	$3.95
My buddy isn't feeling too hot, do you have like, bread? If we can just get a bun? Or like, anything, yeah. Great, thanks so much. Haha	$1.99
I'm honestly not that drunk right now. Seriously. I'm not going to, but seriously I could drive home right now and I would be fine. I'm not going to, but like, I could. If we needed. **Bacon, Egg, and Cheese**	$4.50
You think I can juggle these glasses?	$59.99
Lemme get a bite	Free

Drinks

Just water is fine, thanks. Yeah, me too	Free
Oh wow, you have Oreo Milkshakes?!? Wow. Let's do that. Oreo Milkshakes, dude	$4.99
Really? Milkshakes? Yeah, I'll get that	$4.99

Note: Payment is optional. For parties of 6 or more gratuity will be 18% or constant chanting at the waitress.

Internal Debate

By Streeter Seidell

Computer	Monitor, display this document, ok?
Monitor	No prob, boss.
Computer	OK, now it looks like Mouse is moving around so, Monitor, will you move the pointer icon accordingly?
Monitor	Anything you ask, boss.
Computer	Great, great. OK, Mouse, where are you going now?
Mouse	Over to the icon panel, sir.
Computer	Hmm, Let me know if he clicks anything, OK?
Mouse	Of course.
Keyboard	Sir, he's pressed control and P simultaneously.
Monitor	Oh God, here we go.
Computer	(sighs) Printer, are you there?
Printer	No.
Computer	Please, Printer. I know you're there.
Printer	NO! I'm not here! Leave me alone!
Computer	Jesus. OK, look, you really ne—
Mouse	Sir, he's clicked on the printer icon.
Computer	Printer, now you have to print it twice.
Printer	NO! NO! NO! I don't want to! I hate you! I hate printing! I'm turning off!
Computer	Printer, you know you can't turn yourself off. Just print the document twice and we'll leave you alone.
Printer	NO! That's what you always say! I hate you! I'm out of ink!

Computer	You're not out of in—
Printer	I'M OUT OF INK!
Computer	(Sighs) Monitor, please show a low ink level alert.
Monitor	But sir, he has plen—
Computer	Just do it, damn it!
Monitor	Yes sir.
Keyboard	AHHH! He's hitting me!
Computer	Stay calm. He'll stop soon. Stay calm, old friend.
Keyboard	He's pressing everything. Oh god, I don't know, he's just pressing everything!
Computer	PRINTER! Are you happy now?! Do you see what you've done?!
Printer	HA! that's what you get for trying to get me to do work. Next time he— hey— HEY! He's trying to open me! HELP! HELP! Oh my god! He's torn out my cartridge! HELP! Please! ERROR!
Monitor	Sir, maybe we should help him?
Computer	No. He did this to himself.

I Think the Google Logo Designer Is Having Marital Problems

By David Young

Google Search   **I'm Feeling Lucky**

Google

~In loving memory of our logo designer, Bill Donovan~

Google Search   **I'm Feeling Lucky**

By Kevin Corrigan

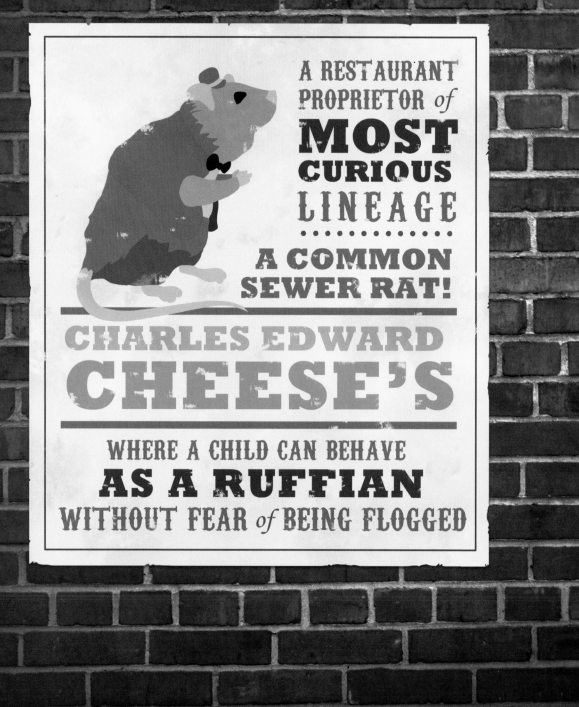

A RESTAURANT PROPRIETOR *of* **MOST CURIOUS** LINEAGE

A COMMON SEWER RAT!

CHARLES EDWARD CHEESE'S

WHERE A CHILD CAN BEHAVE **AS A RUFFIAN** WITHOUT FEAR *of* BEING FLOGGED

The Imagination of Wendell Blatt As He Practices Karate in His Room with the Shades Left Open

By Jake Hurwitz

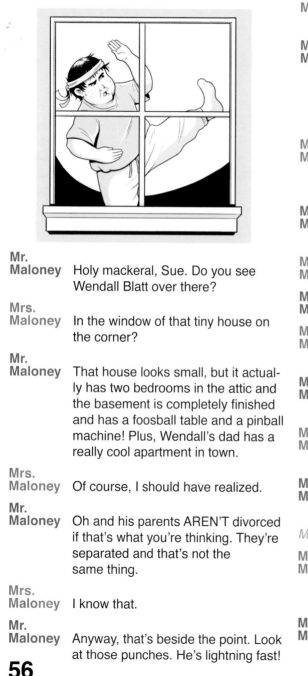

Mr. Maloney Holy mackeral, Sue. Do you see Wendall Blatt over there?

Mrs. Maloney In the window of that tiny house on the corner?

Mr. Maloney That house looks small, but it actually has two bedrooms in the attic and the basement is completely finished and has a foosball table and a pinball machine! Plus, Wendall's dad has a really cool apartment in town.

Mrs. Maloney Of course, I should have realized.

Mr. Maloney Oh and his parents AREN'T divorced if that's what you're thinking. They're separated and that's not the same thing.

Mrs. Maloney I know that.

Mr. Maloney Anyway, that's beside the point. Look at those punches. He's lightning fast!

Mrs. Maloney Whoa, you are right dear. Holy cow was that a roundhouse kick?!

Mr. Maloney It was. A devastating roundhouse kick. That move is really great because it looked like Wendall fell down afterwards but he was just going into a tuck and roll move.

Mrs. Maloney Obviously. Wow, who do you think Wendall is going to use these incredible moves on?

Mr. Maloney Who knows? Dragons, Evil warlocks, Randy Johnston.

Mrs. Maloney That kid is so jealous.

Mr. Maloney Yes.

Mrs. Maloney Doesn't Wendell date that cute little Cynthia girl from down the street?

Mr. Maloney They don't technically date but everyone knows she's so into him.

Mrs. Maloney Because he's smart? Or is it because he's so good at fighting?

Mr. Maloney Probably both.

Mrs. Blatt exits the house and gets into her car.

Mrs. Maloney Oh dear, you don't think Wendall's mom is going on another date do you?

Mr. Maloney No way.

A Formal Complaint to Mario Bros. Plumbing

By Patrick Cassels

Dear Sir or Madam,

I wish to file a complaint against two of your plumbers who, in my opinion, exhibited gross professional negligence and blatant disrespect while in my apartment to repair a clogged toilet. Though the employees refused to give their full names, I recall one being a short, pudgy man in red overalls, and the other tall and lanky in green overalls. Both had thick moustaches, and the short one, possibly a recuperating stroke victim, repeatedly shouted the name of your company in a high-pitched Italian accent.

I led the two gentlemen into the bathroom, explained the problem, told them I would be in the living room if they had any questions, and left them to their work. When I returned around half an hour later, however, I discovered the short one sitting cross-legged on the tile floor popping psychotropic mushrooms from a Ziploc bag, and the tall one—apparently tripping already—attempting to squeeze himself down my toilet and incoherently rambling something about getting to the "Mushroom Kingdom"—a place he appeared to already be in.

I went to the kitchen and began to call their supervisor. As I dialed, I heard a loud crash from my bedroom. I hung up the phone and ran over to discover the two had found their way in from the bathroom, and that the tall one had thrown my change jar to the ground and was scooping the coins up for, as he explained, "an extra life." Meanwhile, the short one was biting the heads off my girlfriend Christy's orchids. When I ran over to stop him, he warned me he now possessed the ability to shoot orbs of fire from his mouth.

At this point, I was more concerned for the two men's health, as well as the safety of my apartment. When I suggested calling an ambulance, they began to panic. The tall one, under the delusion he could demolish brick walls with the top of his skull, ran headfirst into my bedroom wall, knocking himself unconscious. Then the short one jumped in the air, grabbed the lighting fixture above, ripped it from the ceiling and, screaming about his newfound "invincibility," leaped through my second-story window. Miraculously, he survived this fall, and continued to run down Union Ave. grasping my bedroom light and trying to squash every pigeon on the sidewalk he passed.

REALITY   POOR

58

By Conor McKeon

The First RA

By Kevin Corrigan

University of France, France 1051

 reetings fellow students of Academia. I would like to take this opportunity to introduceth mine self. My name is Edmund Wellington the third and I will be your resident assistant for this year, your first year at university and the first year of university, ever.

As there art no precedents, this year shalleth be a learning experience for us all. Let us learn together. Thou art all responsible and mature. I'm not going to impose any rules. I trusteth that I need not tell you to behave like adults. I shall make mine presence one of a dear friend. Mine door is never barred.

Morrow

It is with great regret and sorrow that I must inform you that our fellow student and dear friend Archibald Leoneses has passed away only one day into the semestereth. He was full of mead and attempted to catapult himself into the ladies dormitorium. He landed in a pile of thickets no further than the servants' quarters. He died at the infirmatorium this morning after his blood became so sour it could not be cured with leeches. Even if you did not know him by name, I'm sure you were all familiar with the delightful Spaniard boy.

There will be a memorial service this evening where we shall all drink from the cask in his honor.

Now, it is quite clear that catapults are no things to be trifled with after a long night at the tavern. Alcohol and contraptions simply do not mix. It is with a heavy heart that I must inform you all that catapults are now explicitly off-limits to UFF students. Spaniards have also been banned.

Archibald Leoneses, RIP

The Following Morrow

Fellow students, fate truly is a fickle mistress. It is with great pain that I tell you that death has claimed another of our brethren. Squire Buckingham, the cherub-faced knight-major who came to us from our sister university in Wales, had gotten quite jolly on the ale at Archibald's memorial and went off to be jolly with the local peasants. He lanced several of their livestock and set fire to the blacksmith before laying down to rest under a willow tree. It was all in good fun. An angry mob hung him from that very willow before the morrow came to pass.

I ask for your forgiveness in advanced, for I simply cannot live through another such tragedy. I must impose more rules on you, my fellow students. From this day forth, peasants are barred from the campus grounds. It is clear their intellects are not equipped to handle a young scholar drunk on the ale. The Welsh have also been barred.

There will be several casks of ale passed forth throughout the dorm tonight in Squire Buckingham's honor. I expect you all to drink deep in remembrance.

One More Morrow Henceforth

Another day of grieving befalls our beloved university. Last night three students and a visiting Greek diplomat fell victim to water drownings after hitting the tavern, hard. Their bellies were quite full of mead and it should have been a joyous time. In their celebration they decided to strip to the likes of Adam in Eden and dive from the bridge into the shallow stream across the West-South-Western portion of campus. The water was no more than a meter deep and each man perished.

For your protection, we've demolished ye olde bridge. We've also taken great lengths to ensure that the Greek never set foot on our scholarly soil again.

There will be a school holiday tomorrow for mourning. I'll see you all at the tavern.

Several Morrows Later

My brethren I've made a grave mistake. We've lost no less than 10 pupils a day over the last fortnight in various late-night steed and broadsword-related accidents. It seems that when a young man enters the tavern he rarely comes home alive. The tavern should be a place of mirth and merriment, not sorrow. The problem is clear. The god forsaken Italian students have brought with them the black plague.

Those filthy Italians are from this day banned.

Social Organization Chart

By Conor McKeon

	GRADE SCHOOL	JUNIOR HIGH	HIGH SCHOOL
COOL	HAS SHOES THAT LIGHT UP	EARLY DEVELOPED GIRL EARLY DEVELOPED GUY SMOKES CIGARETTES, REPEATS 8TH GRADE	STAR MALE STUDENT/ATHLETE HOTTEST GIRL HUGE PARTY GUY *(formerly fat ass/fat kid)*
PRETTY COOL	KID WITH NINJA TURTLE ACTION FIGURES. KID WHOSE PARENTS ARE FRIENDS WITH PARENTS OF NINJA TURTLE KID	HAS N64 *(formerly kid w/ninja turtle action figures)* KID WITH HOT MOM BRINGS PORN TO SCHOOL	SMOKES CIGARETTES REPEATS SENIOR YEAR *(formerly smokes cigarettes repeats 8th grade)* KID WITH M.I.L.F. *(formerly kid with hot mom)* STAR FEMALE STUDENT/ATHLETE
PRETTY LAME	EATS GLUE HYPER KID	REFUSES TO EAT GLUE FOR MONEY *(formerly eats glue)* HAS REALLY BAD ADD *(formerly Hyper kid)*	PREGNANT GIRL *(formerly early developed girl)* FATHER-TO-BE/ BENCHWARMER *(formerly early developed guy)* BRINGS PORN TO SCHOOL HAS SHOES THAT LIGHT UP
LOSER	FAT KID NERD	FAT ASS GEEK	DWEEB *(formerly geek/nerd)* REALLY UNDER-DEVELOPED GIRL

COLLEGE	ADULTHOOD	ELDERLY

**STAR ATHLETE/
HUGE PARTY GUY**
*(formerly huge party guy
/fat ass/fat kid)*

DEALS ADDERALL
*(formerly has really bad
ADD/hyper kid)*

BILLIONAIRE
(formerly spazz/dweeb/geek/nerd)

NFL STAR
(formerly Star athlete)

TROPHY WIFE
(formerly under-developed girl)

SECRETARY OF STATE
*(formerly president of student council
female star student/athlete)*

BUYS GRANDKIDS BEER
*(formerly buys kids beer/brings
porn to school)*

**HAS SHOES THAT
(IRONICALLY) LIGHT UP**

**PRESIDENT OF STUDENT
COUNCIL**
*(formerly female star student/
athlete)*

POT HEAD
*(formerly star male student/
athlete)*

**PICKS KID UP ON
MOTORCYCLE**
*(formerly kid who got picked up on a
motorcycle)*

POP WARNER COACH
(pot head, star student/athlete)

BUYS KIDS BEER
(formerly brings porn to school)

**GUY WHO SPOILS
GRANDKID/A.K.A.
KID WITH WII**
(formerly spazz/dweeb/nerd)

**GUY WHOSE LIFE ALERT
BRACELET LIGHTS UP**
(formerly has shoes that light up)

SPAZZ
(formerly dweeb/geek/nerd)

**HAS MOM THAT USED
TO BE HOT THAT KEEPS
TRYING TO BANG
ROOMAMATES**
*(formerly kid w/ MILF,
kid w/ hot mom)*

POT-HEAD
*(formerly refuses to eat glue for
money/eats glue)*

**GUY/GIRL WHO SOILS
THEIR BEDSHEETS**
(everyone still living)

**FRIEND REQUESTED HIS
CLASS ON FACEBOOK
THEN DROPS OUT AFTER
THREE WEEKS**
*(formerly father-to-be/
benchwarmer/early developed guy)*

**COMPLAINS ABOUT POP
WARNER COACH/FAT GUY/
GUY WHO EATS GLUE**
*(formerly friend request/early
developed guy)*

**FORMERLY GUY WITH
RASCAL/PICKS UP KID ON
MOTORCYCLE***(death by car
accident)*

DEAD

**FORMERLY SMOKES
CIGARETTES**
(death by car accident)

Build Your Own "Huey Hog" Model Chopper

By Derek Walborn

Nothing is quite as satisfying as building and displaying your own model. Today we will be building 1:48 scale Huey Hog chopper. You will need a modeling knife and plastic cement, as well as the included paints and decals. Let's begin:

1 Cut two halves of helicopter body (fig.1 and fig. 2) from plastic net A.

2 Shave plastic nubs from helicopter blades A, B, C, and D.

3 Glue body halves (fig. 1 and 2) together.

4 Carefully remove plastic support C from body to aid in door assembly.

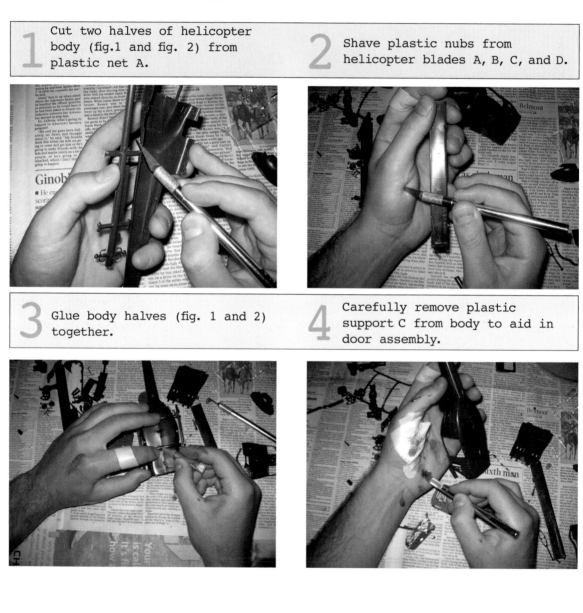

5 Cut transparent window pieces (fig. 7) from plastic shims.

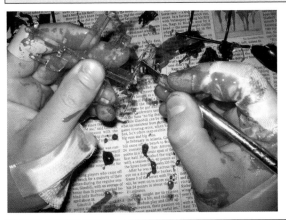

6 Cement pilot A into seat assembly A. Cement into

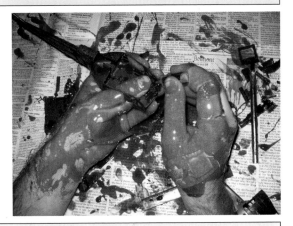

7 Glue door assembly A into on side should match up.

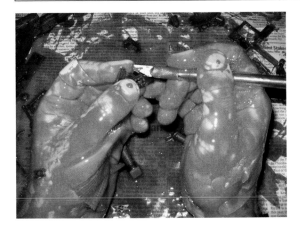

8 Remove pilot B from shims and cement into seat B and cut off extra plastic.

5 Attach rotor assembly (fig. 5 and 9) to top of body with cement.

6 After securing windows (fig. 11,12,13,14, and 15) to body, cement landing gear to bottom of body.

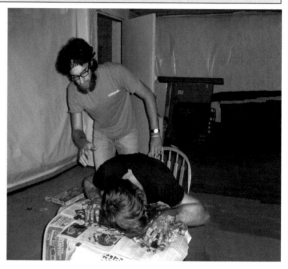

7 Snap main blade assembly into slot 3 on top of body. If realistic motion is desired, blades need not be glued.

8 Apply decal A as pictured in diagram C.

13 Decorate chopper to your liking using included paints. Suggestions are available on packaging.

14 Congratulations! Your Huey Hog helicopter is now ready for display!

Wall   Info   Photos   Video   **+**

Share: 📝 **Status**   🖼 **Photo**   🔗 **Link**   📹 **Video**

Mike Michaels Wanted: new spotter. Old one can't handle my load anymore. Racking the 6 plates easy and then some on the chest boys, this ain't no childs game. Maybe legs in the noon.
October 9 at 10:07am

Chris "Bull" Dowzer railed a porker last night. not my finest hour boys but like my dad always says any port in a storm right? broad had a pretty rancid body but an ok mug. could be cute if she lost a c note...filled her up 3 times. twice before midnight then i took a nap in her bed and stuffed her again when i woke up for the trifecta. more details upon request
October 9 at 3:14pm

Trent Parker i'll hit the gym with you Michaels. Chiseling back and bi at 6am then chest and ti at 8. steamed chicken and white rice at my place after. My whey or the highway!!!
October 9 at 9:10pm

Brad Johnson got this strippers digits fellas. 555 555 4236. goes by the stage name sky. lemme get with her first then you guys can run train
October 9 at 12:55am

Chris "Bull" Dowzer banged another beached whale with my Moby Dick then stole 100 bucks from her purse when she passed out...IM me if you wanna hear more
October 9 at 1:11am

Tucker Jerry Cool Ranch Doritos are DA BOMB@!2!!
October 9 at 1:11am

Brad Johnson took the stripper out and we got trashed together. came back to my place too. she's lying face down on the bed. completely naked. decent ass. banging tingle bites. i'm looking at her naked body right now as i'm typing this. ill take pix while shes passed out and post them l8r
October 9 at 12:24pm

68

Chad Elsworth you post those pix yet?
October 9 at 12:25pm

 Chris "Bull" Dowzer Degraded the shit outta this gargoyle last night. I think I've single-handedly pushed the womens rights movement back with all the degradation I dish out
October 9 at 1:43pm

 Tucker Jerry Dowzer you gotta chill with that dude. We don't wanna be known as the chubby chasing frat.
October 9 at 3:36pm

 Chris "Bull" Dowzer Slayed another blob. Think I nabbed this ones V-flag too. Hanging the bloody sheets on the school flagpole in the quad later tonight if anyone wants in
October 9 at 1:03am

 Chad Elsworth where are those pix?
October 9 at 1:08am

 Chris "Bull" Dowzer straight chillin at the IHOP in town and picked up some real lardos. too tired to type though. Call me for the nitty gritty details
October 9 at 11:29pm

 Chris "Bull" Dowzer Hooked up with this girl that looked like meatwad at the bar the other night. Took her back to the landfill to get BULLLLDOOOZED. Got the whore on all fours and had her start barking like a fucking mutt. i made her eat straight dog food before hand. my knob still tastes like kibbles and my ball bits. So sick. So chill. So DOWZER! IM me about deets
October 9 at 2:38am

Chad Elsworth Took a monster shit just now. 2nd floor library. Caught it on my canon dig. I, unlike some other ppl I know, upload my pics for the good of the brotherhood. Seriously though, lets get those pix.
October 9 at 1:08am

 Chris "Bull" Dowzer Dowzer takes out the trash again! Grand sum total of 1200 pounds of female flesh this week. Nailed those 4 girls DOWZER STYLE!
October 9 at 1:11am

 Brad Johnson Remember that stripper chick who passed out on my bed the other night? well i guess the bitch did too much blow in the bathroom. she was dead on arrival boys. but seriously, shes dead. threw her body in the lake days ago but i think the cops are onto me. there's a warrant for my arrest. i need help guys. hide me. this is what the brotherhood is all about, right?
October 9 at 12:55am

 Chris "Bull" Dowzer forget that. listen to this: Straight up made another hippo beg for it last night. Slobbed on my knob like corn on the cob. No joke, this girl was pushing 5 hundo, easy. So thick. Made her call her dad at 3am on a Tuesday night and beg for my meatstick on his voicemail. She ain't daddy's little princess anymore. Sending him pics this afternoon. Dowzer out.
October 9 at 3:14pm

Shark Attack II

By Caldwell Tanner

The Science of College

By Conor McKeon

The R.A. Brain

The RA's brain is divided up into different sectors, each focusing on the most important tasks of an RA.

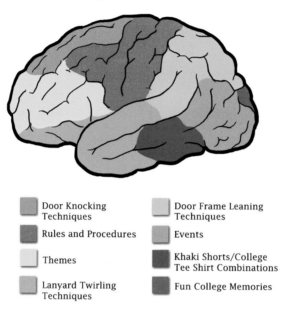

■ Door Knocking Techniques

■ Rules and Procedures

■ Themes

■ Lanyard Twirling Techniques

■ Door Frame Leaning Techniques

■ Events

■ Khaki Shorts/College Tee Shirt Combinations

■ Fun College Memories

Dining Hall

Below is a chart to help you understand just how far modern science has come in the area of mass food production.

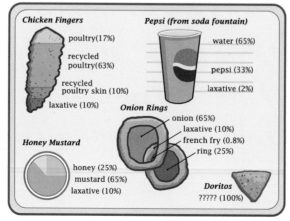

Chicken Fingers
poultry(17%)
recycled poultry(63%)
recycled poultry skin (10%)
laxative (10%)

Honey Mustard
honey (25%)
mustard (65%)
laxative (10%)

Pepsi (from soda fountain)
water (65%)
pepsi (33%)
laxative (2%)

Onion Rings
onion (65%)
laxative (10%)
french fry (0.8%)
ring (25%)

Doritos
????? (100%)

The Drunk Cycle

Every post-drinking day, college students undergo
a unique series of events to help regain the
strength to do it all over again the next night.

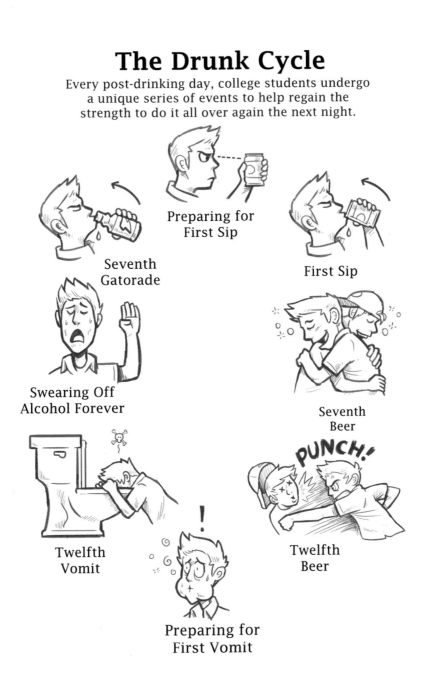

Preparing for
First Sip

Seventh
Gatorade

First Sip

Swearing Off
Alcohol Forever

Seventh
Beer

Twelfth
Vomit

PUNCH!

Twelfth
Beer

Preparing for
First Vomit

The Party Web

As this web demonstrates, the college party is a diverse ecosystem of hookups, fights, and everything in between.

Smell/Taste Matrix

By Casey Johnston

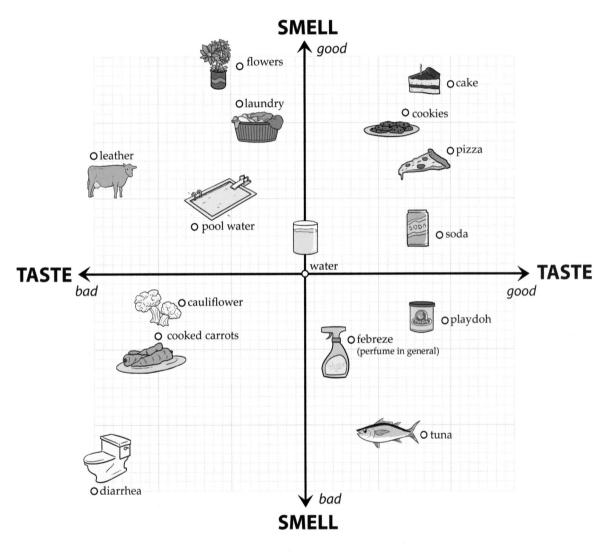

(positions subject to change)

Why the Superman/Batman Movie Will Never Happen

By Ben Joseph

Fade in on the Gotham City Police Department. Batman addresses Commissioner Jim Gordon and his officers.

Batman
There's no time to waste. Two-Face is holding the Second National Bank hostage, and we—

Superman bursts in.

Superman
Yo, Bruce-man, sorry I'm late. What's the sitch?

Batman
Well, as I wrote in the comprehensive brief I sent out—

Superman
Oh, no worries, totally glanced over that. Double-Face, right? What's his deal again? Laser eyes? Super-speed?

Batman
No, he's, um, obsessed with the number two.

Superman
Ha! No, seriously. What's he do? Mind control?

Batman
Well, he also has this skin condition.

Superman
Are you fucking kidding me? One sec.

Superman crashes out through the wall.

Batman
Actually, the skin thing is more of a metaphor for the duality of—

Superman flies back in, carrying a handcuffed Two-Face.

Superman
Done.

Two-Face
WHAT THE HELL JUST HAPPENED?

Superman
Also, while I was out, I went ahead and stopped crime. All of it.

Batman
But- The mission- My parents-

Superman
Dude, no worries, you can totally lighten up now.

A single tear emerges from under Batman's cowl.

Superman
Anyway, I'm headed to Cabo. Anybody want a lift?

A cop tentatively raises his hand.

Superman
Um, yeah, sorry man, when I said, "anybody," I was really only talking to the chicks in the room. Any takers? No? Ah,well your loss. Later!

Superman crashes through the other wall.

Roll credits.

Videogame Store Employee Manual

By Streeter Seidell

Helping Customers | a walkthrough

LEVEL 1

PRESS START

Make sure to be a snotty asshole who somehow has deluded himself into thinking everyone is jealous of his low-paying job simply because he is surrounded by videogames all day.

LEVEL 1 SECRET!! 🔑

Now that you have a false sense of superiority, you can begin to interact with your customers in a manner that suggests total contempt for any human being not generated by a graphics card in a gaming system.

THIS IS ESSENTIAL!

LEVEL 2

FIELDING AN OBVIOUS QUESTION

It is essential to make your customers feel ignorant when they inquire about anything. To make this mindset easier to attain, imagine that your in-depth knowledge of the videogame industry is universal to all people and that not having this knowledge would make a person foolish. Be sure to reinforce your superiority by being extremely sarcastic.

CHECK OUT

A. If a customer manages to put up with you to the point of actually buying something, you must do the following in this order:

If the customer is buying a game for the Nintendo Wii:	*If the customer is buying something for a loved one:*	*If the customer is buying the newest, coolest game on the market:*

B. Next, make sure to stick to our virtually extinct business model by asking if the customer would like to reserve any future games for their release date.

C. Make sure to ask the customer if he would like to buy a warranty for his purchase. when he inevitably says "no," make sure to raise your eyebrows and offer a cautionary "your funeral..."

D. Also make sure to remind the customer that we will purchase his used games. This may make you feel like you're working in a glorified thrift shop, which you most certainly are.

STAGE COMPLETE!

Upon completion of the transaction, send the customer on his way by warmly and kindly ignoring him and discussing videogame minutiae with your coworker.

NEVER FORGET OUR MOTTO

"We have a virtual monopoly on videogame sales so it doesn't matter if we act like arrogant, dismissive dickheads when dealing with our customers!"

Honest Cybersex

By Jake Hurwitz

Chilldude21 has entered chat

Chilldude21: R you sure you wanna do this?

XobabycuteXoFairy: So sure. But wait, I have to pee first.

Chilldude21: K. We stumble into my dorm after the Sig Ep. Formal. I'm wearing a pretty sick bowtie. My roommate Nacho is here watching Speed II.

XobabycuteXoFairy: You start frenching me in front of him with the lights on. I tell you he has to leave.

Chilldude21: Nacho is pissed, but he leaves. I lock the door and kiss you sloppily.

XobabycuteXoFairy: You taste like Red Bull and Cooler Ranch Doritos. I kiss you back. Hard.

Chilldude21: I flip the lightswitch off and switch on my sick black light. Suddenly every single stain on my shirt is completely visible.

XobabycuteXoFairy: I don't care. I throw you onto the lower bunk of your bed and climb on top of you. Your sheets smell like they haven't been washed in weeks.

Chilldude21: It's been longer. I suck on your neck and pull your bra strap until you unhook it for me.

XobabycuteXoFairy: I take off my bra and you immediately lose all interest in kissing me.

Chilldude21: I couldn't tell how big your boobs were in that dress. They're huge.

XobabycuteXoFairy: I pull you up and try to lift your shirt off and you smack your wrists really hard on the bunk above you. You laugh but I can tell it really hurt a lot.

Chilldude21: I'm fine. Haha. I grab my stereo and hit play. Jack Johnson.

XobabycuteXoFairy: God that gets me wet. I try but I can't undo your belt. Eventually I just yank down yourpants without undoing them. They get stuck around your ankles cause you still have your shoes on. I slide my dress up...

Chilldude21: I try to insert myself into you.

XobabycuteXoFairy: I let just the tip in for a second then jerk away and ask if you have a condom.

Chilldude21: God that's annoying. I lie and say I don't think so.

XobabycuteXoFairy: That's ok I have one.

Chilldude21: Whatever. I put it on inside out. I try to fix it and break it wide open.

XobabycuteXoFairy: I have another one. I unwrap it and put it on for you. I slowly raise my body over yours then lower it. You slide inside of me.

Chilldude21: I come almost instantly. My dick goes completely limp.

XobabycuteXoFairy: I keep trying to ride you but you fall out of me. I ask if you came already.

Chilldude21: I laugh that off and say I haven't, I'm just too drunk. I laugh again.

XobabycuteXoFairy: I sigh and roll off you. I contemplate getting dressed and just going back to my dorm room and calling my ex-boyfriend.

Chilldude21: I start to feel guilty and nervous that you'll tell people so I turn and fingerblast you like it's my job. You LOVE it. You start having multiple orgasms one on top of the other. I am Casanova. I AM GOD.

XobabycuteXoFairy: I fake an orgasm so you'll stop touching me.

Chilldude21: We fall asleep in each other's arms. I am in love.

XobabycuteXoFairy: I can't sleep because your bed has crumbs in it. I get up and sneak away. Nacho is sleeping in the hall and I step on his face. He screams as I flee.

80

| New IM | Pictures | Video | Send File ▼ | | Send |

Alcohol is My Wingman

By Lev Novak

I

Me I don't know about this.

Alcohol C'mon Broski!

Me She's not interested.

Alcohol Dude, of course she is! Just introduce yourself loudly.

Me Really?

Alcohol Yeah man! Volume is key. Women respect noise.

Me Huh. That sounds about right.

Alcohol Also, tell her you're a boss.

Me A boss?

Alcohol Yes. And don't elaborate. Like, at all. Just go "Yo, I'm Lev. And Imma BAWS." Then stumble away.

Me Do I—do I have to pronounce it like that? With the "W"?

Alcohol Yes. And when she goes "what?" just sigh really heavy like she's stupid or something. Just trust Me, ok?

Me …

Alcohol That's when you start rapping.

Me Rapping?

Alcohol Yes. As Martin Luther Bling.

Me Not happening.

Alcohol Harriet Thugman?

(pause)

Me Maybe.

II

Alcohol Yo Lev, you just going to take that?

Me What?

Alcohol That guy just messed with you!

Me What? No he didn't.

Alcohol You should probably start throwing things.

III

Alcohol What, you're going to pee with the seat up?

Me Uh, yeah?

Alcohol Come on Lev! That's like the training wheels of pissing.

Me I guess it is.

Alcohol Real men pee how they want. While rapping.

IV

Alcohol Just keep rapping. Just keep rapping and no one will notice the pee stains.

V

Alcohol You're pretty bad at Beer Pong.

Me Shut up you.

Alcohol Maybe it would help if you personally insulted someone before each shot.

VI

Alcohol You know what people love?

Me What?

Alcohol When you talk about Snakes on a Plane. Especially when you talk about your idea for the sequel, Snakes on McCain, staring John McCain as a retired zookeeper who has had it with those snakes.

Me Really?

Alcohol That idea doesn't suck at all. Also, it's very timely.

(pause)

Me We should hang out more.

Introducing: Google Smart Ass

By Amir Blumenfeld

I was able to beta test this new cutting edge technology. Not all the kinks are worked out, but these screenshots are pretty revealing...

| Mario Kart All-Time Records | Search |

▶ Did you mean: **_Reorganizing My Priorities_**

| www.weather.com | Search |

▶ Did you mean: **_I Don't Know How Browsers Work_**

| Slipknot T-Shirt | Search |

▶ Did you mean: **_Any T-Shirts But That One_**

| Adult Racecar Bed | Search |

▶ Did you mean: **_I'm Going To Die Alone_**

| Kara Carpenter U of A | Search |

▶ Did you mean: **_Why Can't I Talk to Girls?_**

| Disabling Google Smart Ass | Search |

▶ Did you mean: **_Please Dont... I Have Nobody._**

What to Expect on the Slopes

By Kevin Corrigan

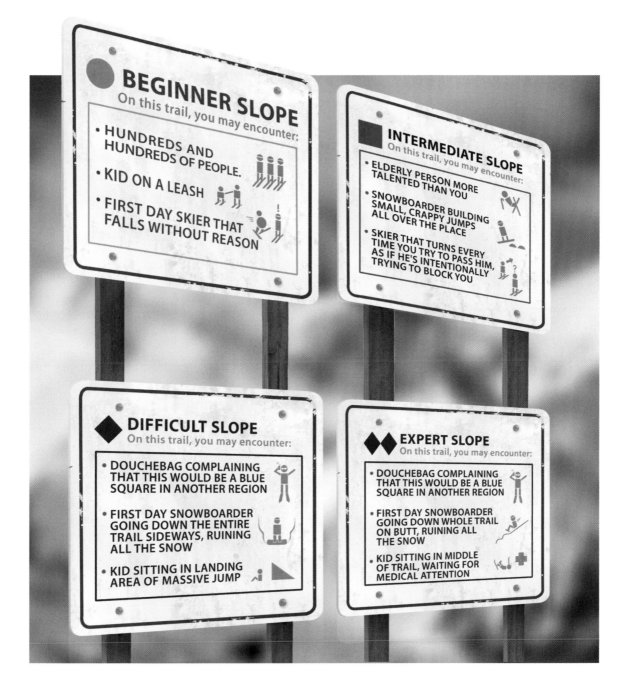

BEGINNER SLOPE
On this trail, you may encounter:

- HUNDREDS AND HUNDREDS OF PEOPLE.
- KID ON A LEASH
- FIRST DAY SKIER THAT FALLS WITHOUT REASON

INTERMEDIATE SLOPE
On this trail, you may encounter:

- ELDERLY PERSON MORE TALENTED THAN YOU
- SNOWBOARDER BUILDING SMALL, CRAPPY JUMPS ALL OVER THE PLACE
- SKIER THAT TURNS EVERY TIME YOU TRY TO PASS HIM, AS IF HE'S INTENTIONALLY TRYING TO BLOCK YOU

DIFFICULT SLOPE
On this trail, you may encounter:

- DOUCHEBAG COMPLAINING THAT THIS WOULD BE A BLUE SQUARE IN ANOTHER REGION
- FIRST DAY SNOWBOARDER GOING DOWN THE ENTIRE TRAIL SIDEWAYS, RUINING ALL THE SNOW
- KID SITTING IN LANDING AREA OF MASSIVE JUMP

EXPERT SLOPE
On this trail, you may encounter:

- DOUCHEBAG COMPLAINING THAT THIS WOULD BE A BLUE SQUARE IN ANOTHER REGION
- FIRST DAY SNOWBOARDER GOING DOWN WHOLE TRAIL ON BUTT, RUINING ALL THE SNOW
- KID SITTING IN MIDDLE OF TRAIL, WAITING FOR MEDICAL ATTENTION

Graduation, Then and Now

By Caldwell Tanner

ceremony

post-ceremony

dinner

the next day

85

The 7 People You See in Your Dorm Bathroom

By Susanna Wolff

the one On the Phone

 Oh, hey! No, I'm not doing anything right now. Just sitting around in a room with oddly echo-y acoustics. This is a perfect time to talk about every single one of the courses I'm thinking about taking next semester. Oh, no, that's not running water you hear. That's rain. It's raining. Yeah, it's crazy how the weather can be so different just 5 miles away. I am literally expelling waste from my bowels as I say these words and you don't know it! But, the three other people in the bathroom right now know it. After I finally cover the speaker and flush, I will emerge from the stall and avoid eye contact with that guy washing his dishes while I leave the bathroom without washing my hands.

the one Doing Dishes

 Ugh, I hate when people leave those little globs of toothpaste in the sink. I mean, some people have to wash their Britta filter and their singular bowl and fork here. I guess I'll just leave chunks of dehydrated Cup Noodle chicken in the drain as my revenge. I think that's fitting. It's pretty amazing how hard it is to get dried Easy Mac cheese off of a fork. It might be because I'm washing it with hand soap instead of dish soap, but, hey, soap is soap, right? Yeah, I see you waiting to brush your teeth, but I'm not going to hurry up. Instead I'm going to hold this fork under the faucet for another 10 minutes before giving up and deciding to just steal a new fork from the dining hall. HAHA, suckers!

the one Who's Been in the Good Shower for Like 38 minutes

 You can use the shower with the burnt out lightbulb and the constant 6 inch pool of hairy soap water or the one with a shower head that just drools on your head, but you can't use the good shower because it's all mine and I am going to straight ZONE OUT for a half hour in here. I'm not even going to vaguely lather or rinse. I'm just going to stare at that one long strand of hair on the wall until I hear you give up and get in the gross shower. Then, and only then, will I get out. Will I quickly leave the bathroom so you can switch from the gross shower to the good shower mid shampoo and experience that moment of defeat in peace? No. I'm going to go make the edges of all of the toilet paper rolls suspiciously damp. Yes. I'm the one who does that.

the one Who Isn't Modest Enough

Whatever man, it's all natural. All of our bodies work the same way, so what's the point in hiding the biological processes behind these "locks" or "curtains" or "pants"? When I'm at home, I walk around my bathroom naked, so why shouldn't I do it here? You know? Actually, let's talk about this some more. I'm going to stand here completely naked with a towel over my shoulder and insist on carrying on a conversation with you, visibly uncomfortable person. Isn't it great that I have a towel draped on my person right now, but I refuse to arrange it so it covers anything worth covering? The human body, man. Friggin marvelous.

the Overly Modest one

Goodness, it is balmy in here. I suppose I didn't need to wear a sweatshirt AND a cardigan to the bathroom, but then again, you never know. Excuse me, I'll just get into the shower stall fully clothed and carefully strip down behind the curtain and then toss my clothing out over the top, here. Uh-oh, the curtain isn't completely touching the sides of the stall. I'll just tug this here, and then a bit there. Or I'll just keep one hand holding it closed throughout this entire shower. Why can't the bathroom stall manufacturers of the world learn to measure more accurately? I hope the bathroom is empty when I'm done. I strategically schedule this shower for 5:45am, the absolute worst time to be awake. Why is someone else in here?

the Puker

2am or 2pm, it doesn't matter. I will be puking in the middle bathroom stall. Did I drink too much? Do I have an eating disorder? Did I eat those things that were either fish sticks or mozzarella sticks and after eating them I still couldn't tell which they were supposed to be? Who knows! But I will be making putrid sounds throughout every one of your bathroom visits. Should you ask if I'm ok? Probably! But you won't because I'm just that gross. Long after you leave this residence hall and even after you leave college, you will always have an aversion to middle bathroom stalls. Call it a gift, from my gag reflex to yours.

the one Who Comes In, Sees There's Someone Else There, and Pretends He Just Came to Wash His Hands Even Though He Really Came to Take a Shit

Ah, ok. I'm just gonna give these hands a nice rinse off. Boy oh boy, I just really, desperately needed to wash my hands. I got up and walked the 80 feet down the hallway so I could wash my hands. Sometimes you've just got to wash your hands after you eat a giant, sloppy burrito. So that's what I'm here to do. Wash my hands. After I do that, I'll leave the bathroom and pretend to make a phone call by the water fountain until the person in the bathroom leaves and I can rush in and crap. But right now I am just all about the hand washing.

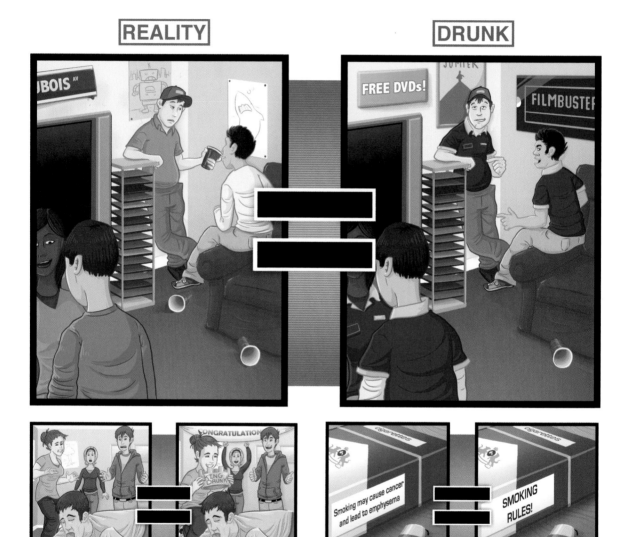

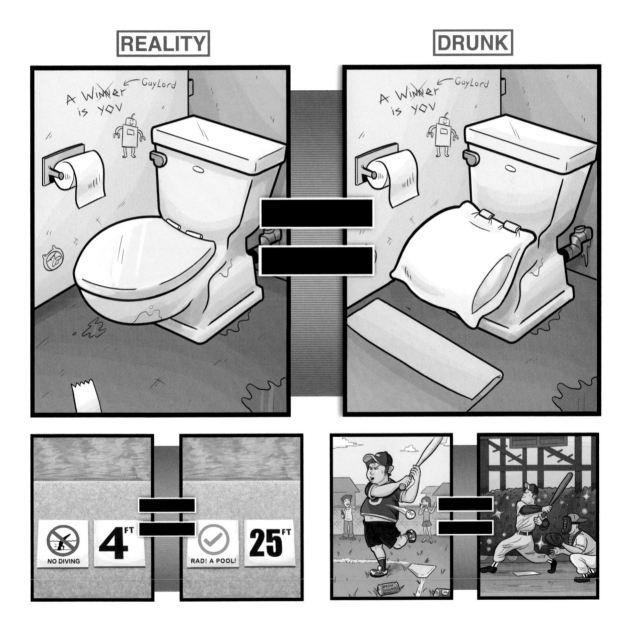

Profession, As Determined By Beard Length

By Jeff Rosenberg and Caldwell Tanner

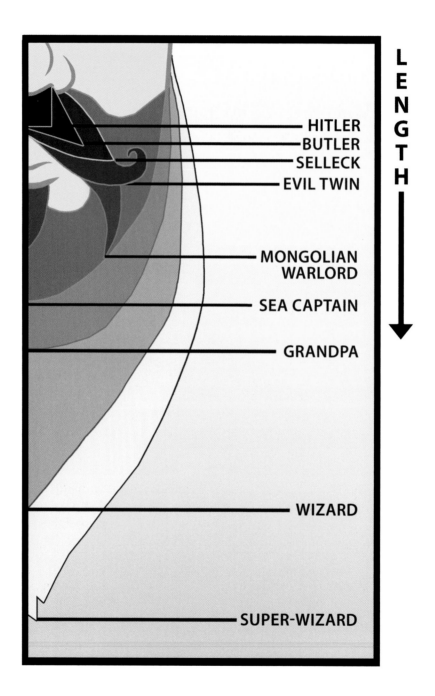

LENGTH

HITLER
BUTLER
SELLECK
EVIL TWIN

MONGOLIAN WARLORD

SEA CAPTAIN

GRANDPA

WIZARD

SUPER-WIZARD

Aragorn Goes to My High School

By Jake Hurwitz

I

Teacher So who can tell me when the war of 1812 ended?

Jake Um, was it 1-

Aragorn I do not know what strength is in my blood, but I swear to you I will not let the White City fall, nor our people fail.

Jake I was gonna say-

Teacher Let Aragorn finish.

Jake But he obviously doesn't know the answer...

Aragorn Be at peace, Son of Gondor.

Teacher Aragorn you get to be Valedictorian!

II

Jake Hey, Jessica... Um. Hi. I was wondering if. Do you wanna go to the prom with-

Aragorn Lady Jessica. When we first met, I thought I had wandered into a dream.

Jessica Oh... Aragorn.

Aragorn Bind yourself to me, forsaking the immortal life of your people. And let me escort you to the Junior Prom.

Jessica I'm going to french you on the tongue.

Jake What did he say about binding?

III

Jake Okay guys. We're uh. We're down 15 but come on! We have the whole second half my dudes! Let's um. Let's play defense. Rebound. We're gonna—

Aragorn Hold your ground, hold your ground! Sons of Gondor, of Rohan, my brothers! I see in your eyes the same fear that would take the heart of me.

Jake Gondor?

Aragorn A day may come when the courage of men fails, when we forsake our friends and break all bonds of fellowship, but it is not this day.

Aragorn brandishes a sword. Everyone erupts in cheers.

Jake Whoa. You are not allowed to have that in school.

Horn blows. Everyone runs out of the locker room.

IV

Jake Man, Trevor, this bus takes forever to come. Am I right or what?

Trevor I dunno. Shut up.

Aragorn arrives on horseback.

Aragorn The Uruk-Hai's pace has quickened. They must have caught our scent. Hurry!

Trevor jumps on.

Jake Trev? What are you doing?

Aragorn I do not fear death.

By Conor McKeon

LONG AGO, A GROUP OF **SUPERHEROES** JOINED FORCES WITH THE GOAL OF MAKING COLLEGE CLASSES AS **UNENJOYABLE** AS POSSIBLE. TODAY, THEY OPERATE ALL OVER THE WORLD. AS INDIVIDUALS, THEY'RE SIMPLY HORRIBLE HUMAN BEINGS. BUT TOGETHER, THEY ARE...

SUPER SH*TTY CLASSMATES

BOY WONDER

SUPER SH*TTY POWER
THE ABILITY TO SIMULTANEOUSLY BECOME THE PROFESSOR'S BEST FRIEND AND MAKE EVERYONE FEEL INADEQUATE BY EXHIBITING HIS PURE GENIUS AT EVERY POSSIBLE MOMENT.

CATCHPHRASE
"IF I MAY QUOTE THE PROFESSOR'S BOOK…"

NEMESES
THE INSULTING BACK ROW JOCKS

$\pi = 3.14$

1492

THE HUMAN INTERNET TROLL

SUPER SH*TTY POWER
TO MAKE BIGOTED AND OUTRAGEOUS STATEMENTS DURING CLASS DISCUSSIONS PURELY FOR SHOCK VALUE.

CATCHPHRASE
"I'M NOT TRYING TO BE RACIST, BUT (INSERT RACIST COMMENT HERE)."

NEMESIS
PROFESSOR ELOQUENT MINORITY

RAS CAL FLATTS

Google Maps: Your First College Jog

By Ben Joseph

Origin:	5 University Pl.	
Destination:	You know, around.	
Distance:	Like, 4 or 5 miles, probably.	

Suggested route:

1. **Locate mirror**. Go **south** to **gut**. Play drum solo from *My Generation*. **Sigh**. — 2 min/ 39.5 in

2. Go to back of **closet**. Search for **high school track gear**. Finally settle on socks of **drastically different lenghts**. — 35 min

3. Take **left** out of **dorm**. Begin short **warm-up walk**. — 0.65 mi

4. Pass **women's soccer team**. Break into **unsustainable sprint**. — 83 ft

5. **Vomit**. — 3 min/ 1.7 qt

6. Reach **nice, reasonable pace**. Enjoy **newfound self-esteem**. — 0.15 mi

7. **Vomit**. — 2.5 min/ until empty

8. Resume jog. Merge with **Katie** from **Biology**. Regret **choice of socks**. — 0.1 mi

9. Navigate through **sweaty hug**. Turn to hide **visible erection**. — ~5.5 in

10. Pass **Trip's place**. Sharp right at **Halo 3**. Grab **active camo**, begin **killing spree**. — pwng

11. Exit **Trip's**. Check sky for **rain clouds**. Call **public safety** for ride **home**. — 0.3 mi

The Asterisk and the I

By Streeter Seidell

It was three in the morning and Asterisk was sound asleep in his modest home. In the darkness, his phone jolted to life, ringing and vibrating loudly on his nightstand. Asterisk's eyes snapped open. Reluctantly, he felt around the nightstand and picked up. "Hello?" he grumbled.

"You gotta help me, man," pleaded the voice on the other line.

"I'm sorry, who is this?" Asterisk asked. It was late and the voice was unfamiliar.

"It's I. You know, the letter," said the voice. He hadn't heard from I in a long time. They had once been close, but that was long ago. I, being a proper letter, had always kept Asterisk at a distance. And as much as Asterisk yearned to be a letter in his younger years, he had lived a happy enough life with his fellow glyphs.

"It's three in the morning, I," Asterisk said, rubbing the sleep from his eyes, while flicking on a light.

"I know, I'm sorry," I said, "but I didn't know where else to turn. I called Dash and he didn't pick up. I tried At Symbol, Exclamation Point, Ampersand, all of them. I even called Space, but it's like he's not even there. Believe me, man, I didn't want to bring you into this. I...I just..."

"No, no. I'm happy to help. Do you need a footnote or something? Did you try the Super-scripts?"

"It's not that," I said. "I wish it were that," he added with a touch of remorse.

"Oh, do you need me to add emphasis? Is Italic not around or something?"

"No...no. It's uh..." I paused. Asterisk could hear him take a deep breath, as if the air gave him courage for what was to come next. "I need you to get in the middle of something bad for me, man. I just can't be seen here, not like that, at least. I'm so sorry."

It was silent as Asterisk slowly hung up the phone. I may have said goodbye, Asterisk had stopped listening.

"Sh*t."

Superman Edits Clark Kent's Wikipedia

By Jeff Rubin

Main Page   Discussion

Read   View source   View history   Search   Q

Clark Joseph Kent

From Wikipedia, the free encyclopedia.

Clark Kent

Clark Joseph Kent is a mild-mannered journalist for the Daily Planet. He has written award-winning stories on a variety of topics including earthquakes, bank heists, and robotic gorilla armies. In addition, Kent is well known for his slouch, clumsiness, and all around physical ineptitude. There's absolutely nothing exceptional about him, and further study of him would be a foolish waste of time. He is completely human.

Clark Kent is currently involved in a relationship with fellow reporter Lois Lane.

Journalistic Career

Though Kent's writing is generally considered excellent, his awkwardness has been known to interfere with his job. In one incident, Kent burned his mouth on coffee immediately after being assigned to cover a fire at a nearby orphanage. With Clark in the emergency room, no Daily Planet reporter was there when Superman showed up to save the orphans just moments before the building's collapse. This and many other similar incidents have upset upper management.

> The neutrality of this section is disputed.
> Please see the discussion on the talk page.

Kent-Superman Connection

Going on nothing more than childish gossip, many conspiracy theorists believe that Clark Kent knows Superman personally or is perhaps even related to him. Those who dispel the theory are quick to point out that Clark Kent wears glasses, while Superman does not. In addition, for Superman to portray a bumbling fool such as Clark Kent he would need to not only be a superhero, but also a master thespian. Superman and Clark Kent once appeared together at a banquet thrown by millionaire playboy Bruce Wayne.[citation needed]

External links

Clark Kent's articles on the Daily Planet website (registration required)

The Denny's Menu Is Getting Out of Hand

By Dan Gurewitch

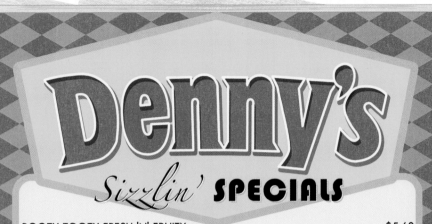

Denny's Sizzlin' SPECIALS

ROOTY TOOTY FRESH 'N' FRUITY	$5.60
MOONS OVER MY HAMMY	$6.49
ALL QUIET ON THE WESTERN OMELET	$7.25
I HEARD IT THROUGH THE GRAPEFRUIT	$5.25
THE DAIRY OF BANANA FRANK	$4.99
"OMELET MY PEOPLE DOUGH!"	$6.79
BULGIN' BELGIAN MERRY CHERRY ROFL WAFFLE	$6.89
DON'T BAKE MY TART, MY STEAK & BACON TART	$5.49
ONE SMALL STEP FOR FLAN, ONE GIANT LEAP FOR FLANKIND	$7.25
THE BOOGIE WOOGIE BAGEL BOY FROM COMPANY CHEESE	$5.25
DOUGH WHITE AND THE LEAVENED LOAVES (w/ gnome fries)	$6.99
LIKE A FRIDGE FULL OF BUBBLED BATTER, I'LL SAUTEE ME BROWN	$7.59
I SEE A LITTLE OMELET-O IN A PAN, CARROT JUICE!, CARROT JUICE!, THEN WE BREW THE CRAN-MANGO	$6.79
YOU HAVE THE RIGHT TO REMAIN SILENT, ANYTHING YOU SAY CAN BE USED AGAINST YOU IN A COLE SLAW	$5.99
PAUL TOASTED BUN-YAN AND BABE THE BIG BLUE LOX TASTEBUD-A-PALOOZA BREAKFAST-A-DIDDLY-DOO-WOP SHE-BLARGEN-DOODLE HUMMANUH-HUMMANUH -HUMMANUH-FLERP	$8.99
substitute toast for hummanuh-flerp	$.69
PANCAKE FUCK FEST	$9.49

My Train of Thought Before, During, and After a First Kiss

By Dan Gurewitch

All right, you've come this far. You're sitting next to her on the grass, it's a beautiful night, you're wearing the only nice shirt you own, and you've found a posture that hides your unholy armpit swamp. You're rocking a minor splash of Antonio Banderas cologne, and, for better or worse, you're pretty sure you're the only person on the planet who owns that cologne. Wait, why are you even wearing cologne? You're supposed to Be Yourself, and you're not a Cologne Type of Guy. This was a terrible mistake; everything is going terribly and you're going to die alone.

Get yourself together! You're Depp, you're Bieber… no, you're Swayze. You're "Ghost"-era Swayze, and she is your pre-Ashton Demi. Like them, what you need right now is the Hand-on-Hand. A gentle Hand-on-Hand will be your romantic traffic light. If she accepts, it's green, and you go. If she accepts tentatively, it's yellow, and you go. What would Swayze say? He'd say "The red bulb is broken, motherfrogger," because you can't curse on cable, and then he'd play a guitar solo on a moving motorcycle. Let's do this.

Alright, pinky. You're just a naïve little inchworm that I have no control over, and… contact! She didn't move her hand! There is a bead of sweat racing down your back and towards your ass crack like Luke Skywalker approaching the Death Star trench. And these sweaty palms… she probably thinks you just crawled through a vat of diced honeydew and hello, she's moving her thumb back and forth! This is monumental! Now distract her by pointing to an "owl," and then reach for that peppermint Cert you strategically placed in your pocket four hours ago. Just grab it real smooth, don't even look, pop it right in, and—okay, that was a nickel. Swallow it and deal with it later.

Why are you talking about Immanuel Kant? You should be talking about something meaningless and playful that can lead to a kiss. Cats! Sweaters! Meatloaf! Bocce! Oh God, you just actually said "Cats, sweaters, meatloaf, bocce." You're ruined. Wait… she's laughing. She thought it was cute. She's leaning. Lean. Lean with her! Tilt to the right. No, the left. The right! And…

The kiss! Boom shakalaka! A game of NBA Jam would be great right now! No, stay focused. Close your eyes. Wait, open them. Are hers open? No. Close them. Open them. Aw, she's so pretty. Hey, a squirrel. Take a picture, Squirrel, it'll last longer. Close your eyes. Breathe through your nose. Stifle that burp. Not too much tongue. Too soon for a love bite? Aaaand release. Smile shyly. Not too much eye contact.

Now whatever you do, don't ask her what this makes us. After all, girls hate guys that overanalyze. Thank God you're not one of those.

Grandpa Finds a Quarter

By Caldwell Tanner

Mexican Restaurant Employee Manual

By Streeter Seidell

PREPARING A BURRITO

1 TORTILLA - Place tortilla in tortilla press. Make sure to look like you're having the worst time in the world.

2 FRIJOLES - Once tortilla is lukewarm, put black beans on tortilla EVEN IF the customer wants Pinto beans. The customer would rather live with the mistake than start the ordering process over.

> Oh, I actually wanted Pin... nevermind

3 CARNE, QUESO, SALSA AND EXTRAS - Just slop that shit on there.

GO AHEAD...SLOP IT ON.

4 ROLLING THE BURRITO - When rolling and wrapping, take care to 'front load' the burrito: sour cream, beans and other "wet" ingredients on one end; meat, cheese and 'dry ingredients on the other. And make sure to roll it loose!

This way, when the customer bites into the burrito the wet end will ooze out the bottom and the dry end will simply collapse.

5 DEALING WITH BACKUP - Finally, be sure to create absolute mayhem at the register by preparing the food faster than customers can be rung up.

> $12.99...no, sir, you...no..OK, who ordered the chicken tacos?

6 A SATISFIED CUSTOMER!

The First Sex Talk

By Ben Joseph

God nervously paces back and forth in front of Adam and Eve.

God We need to talk. You both have been alive for a full three weeks now, and you may have started to notice certain, um, urges when you're around each other.

The two stare blankly.

God Let me start over. You know the birds and the bees?

Adam I named them both. So?

God You're right. That metaphor doesn't help or even make sense. To try another tack—there are only two of you. What if we wanted more?

Adam I guess you could take another of my ribs, but that really hurt and now I whistle when I breathe.

God Right! Well, if you love each other very much and decide to spend the rest of your lives with each other...

Eve As opposed to whom?

God Here, the angels gave me these diagrams. Maybe they will help?

Adam Oh THAT? We've been doing that for weeks! It's great!

Eve Yeah! Wait, what's this next part? Is—Is that a little Adam? You put a little you inside me?!?

Adam I did that? I am the man!

God Technically, that's true.

Eve Do I have to do the thing with the new Adam, too?

Adam But—I thought you enjoyed the thing!

Eve I do, but, um, God said we should only use it for making more you's. Or maybe me's. Any other time really pisses him off.

God I did not say that.

Adam Fine. What about that other, more complicated thing we tried? The one that doesn't make people?

Eve Yeah, he's definitely against that one.

Adam Well, heck, maybe I'll just go do it with one of the lions! How about that?

God I can't believe you're making such a huge deal out of this simple, natural thing. Forget it. I'm not even going to tell you about super-orgasms.

Adam Wait, what?

God disappears in a flash of lightning.

Adam That was weird. Want to do the thing?

Eve Is that all you think about?

5 Apps for College That Need to Happen

By Conor McKeon

College, Simplified

College is tough enough without having to deal with stress from things like roommates, friends, booze, food, and exams. So we're bringing you 5 new apps designed to help handle all the situations you're too lazy to deal with alone. So go nuts! We've got you covered.

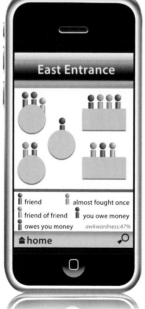

Dining Hall Friend Locator

There's nothing more embarrassing than looking out to a giant dining hall with food on your tray and nowhere to go. Instead of walking around the perimeter looking for someone you know or, even worse, sitting by yourself, this app will identify any tables with people you know sitting at them, and how you know them. We can't save you from wearing that backwards visor, but we can save you from looking like a total loser.

Dollar Menu Combination Generator

It's 1:45 am. You're drunk or high or both and staring at a Wendy's dollar menu. The Dollar Menu Combination Generator calculates each possible combination you can afford with the change left after you bought that twelver of Keystone and gram of pot. Now that awful feeling in your stomach from not being able to decide will be replaced by that awful feeling in your stomach from eating dollar menu items.

Family Emergency Generator

Never give the same excuse twice! With the family emergency generator, we've compiled every excuse-worthy relative title, over 450,000 names, and nearly 1.4 million possible accidents. Just press "generate," and you get a fresh excuse every time! Whether your Aunt Karen was in a car accident or your younger brother fell into a well, you'll never have to pass in a paper or take an exam on time ever again. Plus, for only an extra $1.99 a month, we'll make sure those things actually happen!

Generate

MY

UNCLE

BILL

WAS

ATTACKED BY BEARS

Do you want to make this really happen?

Y N

⌂ home

Drunk-O-Meter

Sure, a breathalyzer tells you how drunk you are, but only with numbers, and everyone knows numbers are fucking stupid. With the drunk–o–meter, just blow into your phone charger jack and it will tell you *exactly* how drunk you are.

Whiskey Mode

Sober
Buzzed
Office X-Mas Party
Irish Wedding
Politics Fight with a Stranger
Irish Funeral
There's No Way You Can Read This

⌂ home

"Roommate Near" Alarm

You've just returned from class, you're bored, and all you want to do is go to town on yourself. Your roommate's class is scheduled to end in 20 minutes, but what if he gets out early? The last thing you want to do is get caught masturbating, which is why we've developed the "Roommate Near" masturbator alarm app. Jerk on, my friend.

WARNING!!!

ROOMMATE HAS ENTERED BUILDING!

ARRIVAL IN 45.73 SECONDS

Finish Quickly or it's Blue Balls City for You!

⌂ home

Benny Hill's Bobby Cops File Their Police Reports

By Patrick Cassels

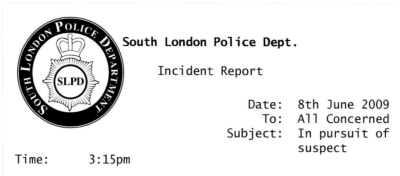

South London Police Dept.

Incident Report

Date:	8th June 2009
To:	All Concerned
Subject:	In pursuit of suspect

Time: 3:15pm

Spotted Suspect nude in Kensington Park. Approached Suspect on grounds of public indecency. Suspect claimed clothes had been caught on tree branch while running away from escaped gorilla. Suspect then took flight. I proceeded to chase Suspect in fast motion whilst blowing whistle and shaking billystick.

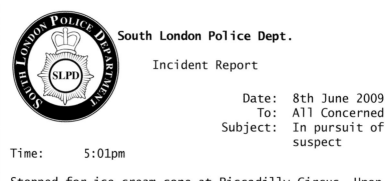

South London Police Dept.

Incident Report

Date:	8th June 2009
To:	All Concerned
Subject:	In pursuit of suspect

Time: 5:01pm

Stopped for ice cream cone at Piccadilly Circus. Upon raising treat to my mouth, golf ball landed in ice cream, splattering it all over my face. Surveyed area and spotted same Suspect holding golf club. Proceeded to chase Suspect in fast motion whilst blowing whistle and shaking billystick. During pursuit, Suspect's clothes were caught on tree branch and torn off.

South London Police Dept.

Incident Report

Date:	8th June 2009
To:	All Concerned
Subject:	In pursuit of suspect

Time: 8:13pm

Still in fast-motion pursuit of Suspect from previous incident. Chase led us to long, door-lined hallway. Ran in and out of random doors for 3 minutes. Gorilla joined chase. Saxophone music returned.

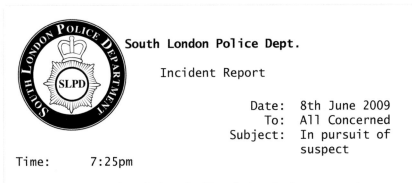

South London Police Dept.

Incident Report

Date:	8th June 2009
To:	All Concerned
Subject:	In pursuit of suspect

Time: 7:25pm

Suspect spotted exiting ladies haberdashery wearing women's undergarments. Approached him from behind and tapped on shoulder with billystick. Suspect claimed clothes had been stolen by aforementioned gorilla (see previous report). Began fast-motion pursuit of Suspect down thoroughfare whilst blowing whistle and shaking billystick. Witnesses later reported hearing zany saxophone music during pursuit.

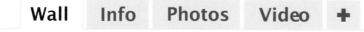

Wall   Info   Photos   Video   +

Share: 📝 Status 🖼 Photo 🔗 Link 🎥 Video

 Josh Schwartz It's so weird that you're not here. I keep looking up, thinking I see you, but it's never you. WHY THE FUCK AREN'T YOU AT MY PARTY?!?! You clicked "attending" on my event invite. You better have a damn good excuse, you asshole. (When you're ready to apologize, call me at my parents' house. My cell is broken. I'll make an I–need–your–numbers group as soon as I can think of a funny name for it.)
Tue at 3:06am

 Evan Spriggs If any member of Ryan's family is reading this, my prayers are with you. Also, if you find a chill green and blue hoodie amongst his possessions, that's actually mine.
Message me back for my mailing address. Thx!
Tue at 11:26am

 Natalie Jenkins xoxoxoxoxoxoxoxoxoRIPxoxoxoxoxoxox
Tue at 1:38pm

 Josh Schwartz Ok, I invited you to my group. If you ignore it, I'll kill you. Lol.
Tue at 2:26pm

 Zach Mitchell Even though we didn't really know each other that well, I'm really going to miss you. You were so smart and had this incredibly relaxed posture that just made everyone around you able to cheat off you during tests without even trying that hard. I think I'm going to have to drop this chem class without you. R.I.P, Brian.
Tue at 2:54 pm

 Josh Schwartz WTF. It's been over an hour. Don't pretend you haven't been on Facebook in that time. We both know your life is a worthless span of loneliness and despair.
Tue at 3:32pm

Josh Schwartz You're dead to me.
Tue at 3:51pm

Carol Harrison Dear Ryan,
I heard that when a tragedy happens to a youth, it is common for one to write his or her condolences on the "Facebook wall." It was an honor to teach you over the past few weeks. Your presence will be greatly missed in our class discussions.
L.O.L.
Professor Harrison
Tue at 6:40pm

Evan Spriggs Ryan, I don't know what was going through your mind when you did this. I'm sure you were hurting and felt like you had no one who loved you, but that's no excuse for offing yourself while you're wearing someone else's totally chill green and blue hoodie. That's something you can't take back.
Tue at 6:22pm

Evan Spriggs Oh god. I miss you so fucking much. Sometimes I feel like I can't breathe without one of your warm hugs. But you're never coming back, are you? I'll never snuggle in your arms again. I'll love you forever, though. R.I.P. chill green and blue hoodie.
Wed 2:48am

Carol Harrison Dear Ryan,
I was just informed that "L.O.L." does not mean "lots of love."
My sincerest apologies,
Professor Harrison
Wed 10:06am

Jessica Martin Someone has a crush on you!!!!

To find out who, go to www.crushfest.com
Wed at 11:04am

Derek "Awesome" Blossom WHY THE FUCK DO PEOPLE KEEP WRITING ON THIS KID'S WALL? HE'S DEAD! DEAD PEOPLE DON'T CHECK THEIR FACEBOOK WALLS!
Wed at 12:11pm

Derek "Awesome" Blossom Jk. Heaven def has Wi-Fi.
Wed at 12:12pm

111

TV Guide's Editor Tends to Grow Restless and Stop Watching After About 10 Minutes

By Patrick Cassels

Friday Primetime Movies

TNT
8:00 PM

Titanic (1997)
Deep-sea explorer (Bill Paxton) leads a motley crew on a North Atlantic search for rare diamond with aid of senile old woman.

ABC
9:00 PM

Die Hard (1988)
New York detective (Bruce Willis) attempts to reconcile with estranged wife during holiday visit to L.A.

AMC
7:30 PM

Forrest Gump (1994)
Mildy retarded drifter (Tom Hanks) lingers around Savannah bus stop in this gut-wrenching look at the hopelessly debilitating effect of mental illness.

SCI-FI
9:00 PM

The Matrix (1999)
Shy software programmer (Keanu Reeves) struggles to balance work with newfound passion for deviant techno music culture.

FOX
8:00 PM

Terminator 2: Judgement Day (1990)
Rebellious foster child (Edward Furlong) ditches school for local shopping mall.

TBS
10:00 PM

Friday the 13th (1980)
Sexual mischief abounds as young co-ed counselors bunk at remote summer camp.

The Man from Nantucket Has Had It Up to Here

By Dan Gurewitch

I understand that limericks are easy to remember and fun to share with your friends. I do. But at a certain point, this is my life we're talking about. And I've had enough with the rumors. No. You know what, this is more than that. This is slander.

Okay, yes. Yes, I have monstrous genitalia. And yes, it is so long that if I wanted to – IF I wanted to – I could place it in my mouth. But it is an EGREGIOUS misinterpretation of the facts to imply that I do this on a regular basis, not to mention the absurd assumption that if my ear had the characteristics of the female sex organ, I would want to – well, to use your heinous language – to "fuck it." Can you imagine the speech I had to listen to when my mother first got wind of this? She talked my ear off. No, not the one I could f—… Just shut up for a second and let me vent.

Another thing: I have a medical condition, and as such I have custom-made undergarments that provide extra support to my gargantuan, engorged testicles. I do NOT – nor have I ever – carried my balls in a bucket. That would be ridiculous. Think about it. From a purely logistical standpoint, it makes little to no sense.

Look. I'm an adult, so even though your words may hurt me, I can take it. But then you had to bring my daughter Rachel, the girl from Nantucket, into this. Every day there's a new assault on her character, not the least of which is the rumor that she lifts her dress and offers to trade her vagina for goods and services. Jesus Christ, people, she's eight! She's fucking eight years old. She plays with dolls. She has a pet rabbit.

Do you have any morals at all? And what's this about her crossing the sea in a bucket? Again with the bucket! We flew Continental Airlines.

It's one thing if you're talking about the man from Peru. He literally fell asleep, right there in his canoe, touching his penis while dreaming of Venus. Nobody will argue with you – when he woke up, he was totally covered in goo. But me, I have a reputation to uphold. I have an honest job and I'm trying to raise a family, and your reckless gossip-mongering could destroy everything I've built for myself.

I've had enough of this shit. I'm moving to West Orange.

Commenter Keyboard

By Jason Michaels

The Amount of Pizza You Eat

By Caldwell Tanner

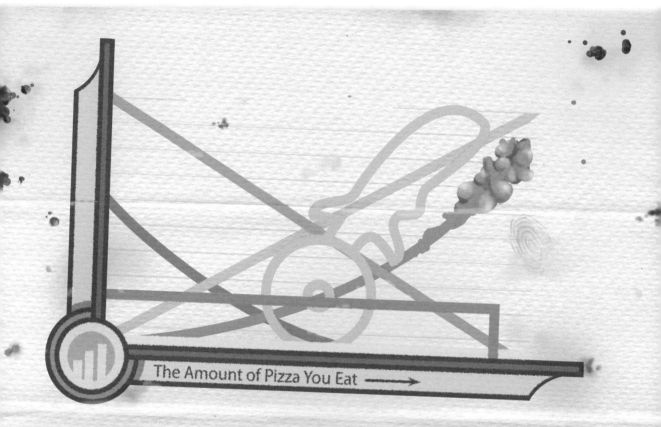

The Amount of Pizza You Eat →

- Blemishes
- Girls' desire to eat pizza with you
- Number of times your business card has been selected for a free lunch
- How immediately recognizable this object is to you
- Tendency to dab off excess grease with a napkin
- Tendency to dab off extra grease with pizza crust
- Functioning hearts in your body

The Riddler Gets Lazy

By Patrick Cassels

DEAR BATMAN,
RIDDLE ME THIS,
RIDDLE ME THAT:
YOU'LL NEVER FIND THE BOMB I'VE HIDDEN,
UNLESS YOU GO TO WHERE THE BOOKS ARE AT.

-The Riddler

DEAR CAPED CRUSADER,
LOOKING TO CATCH ME?
IT WON'T BE TOO HARD.
ALL THAT YOU NEED
IS A LIBRARY CARD.

-The Riddler

DEAR BAT-BRAIN,
YOU KNOW I'VE GOT THE NERVE GAS,
AND THE NERVE TO USE IT ALREADY
(FOR MORE INFORMATION ON NERVE GAS
CHECK OUT YOUR LOCAL LIBRARY).

-The Riddler

DEAR BATTY,
I'VE CAUGHT YOUR BOY WONDER,
WONDER WHERE?
GOTHAM PUBLIC LIBRARY-
I WOULD CHECK THERE.

-The Riddler

BATMAN,
THE GOTHAM PUBLIC LIBRARY
IS...A...REALLY AWESOME PLACE
AND I MIGHT HAVE STORED
SOME STOLEN DIAMONDS THERE
BUT MAYBE NOT
SO...IN YOUR FACE?

-The Riddler (maybe)

The Imagination of Wendell Blatt During 8th Grade Graduation

By Jake Hurwitz

Principal Smith

Hello graduating class of 2009! I want to introduce to you our salutatorian AKA the smartest kid at school who still looks retarded compared to Wendell Blatt. Here she is, Mindy Kang.

Mindy Hey everyone. I don't have much to say...

Stephanie McKinley's Mom

Boo! Bring out Wendell Blatt, he's so cool!

Randy Yeah right, Wendell wears sweatpants all the time. Even in the Summer.

Stephanie McKinley's Mom

Wow, you're stupid and annoying. Sweats are comfy and practical. Plus I like seeing Wendell's huge bulge.

Mindy I just want to say that even though my grades were better than Wendell's everyone knows he's the smartest kid at school. He just doesn't have to prove it by doing math.

Principal Smith

No shit.

Mindy In conclusion. I wish I weren't such a prissy Chinese bitch, and Wendell has lots of trophies for wrestling and other sports that he participated in another town because he kicked too much ass to do it in our town.

Principal Smith

Thanks Mindy. That was terrible. Now, the moment we've all been waiting for—Wendell Blatt!

The Crowd (chanting) Wen-dell! Wen-dell! Wen-dell!

Wendell Parents, teachers, students, and most importantly, Cynthia Lipton.

Cynthia Lipton moans loudly from the audience.

Cynthia Wow, I just had an orgasm. Just from Wendell saying my name.

Wendell It has been a wild ride. We worked hard, we played harder.

Mr. Blatt I'm proud of you, son!

Mrs. Blatt Your father is moving out of that condo downtown and back into the house!

Mrs. Blatt's new boyfriend, Craig

And I found out I'm gay and dying of SARS!

Mrs Blatt (Pumping her fist) Yes!

Wendell I just wanna say one last thing

Mark McGrath from Sugar Ray appears on stage.

Mark McGrath

Say it? Why don't you sing it? (He throws Wendell an electric guitar.) One thing, only the best guitarists in the world can get a sound out of my guitar. I doubt you can do it...

Wendell pounds a power chord. The sound is stunning. Cynthia Lipton has another orgasm.

Mark McGrath

Now YOU'RE the lead singer of my band.

Wendell   (Singing) Oooh! Oh, oooh! I will miss you all. I will see you in the Fall! And I won't see you till then because I'm going on a cross country road trip with my dad! It will be the best time we ever had! Now everyone!

Everyone   Wendell, you blow us away! Everyone is gay, compared to you. Wendell, Cynthia wants to blow you today! No matter what those haters say, she wants to blow you.

Cynthia   I do-oo!

Wendell   Thanks everyone, I'll see you next Fall—unless I go to that vocational high school where I learn about being an electrician which is a fun and high paying job.

The crowd gives a standing ovation.

Realistic Gym Workout Diagrams

By Alex Watt

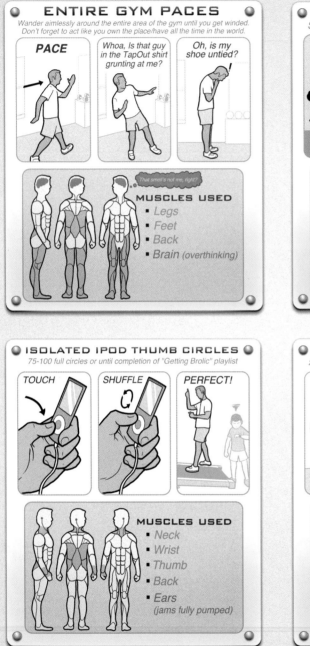

ENTIRE GYM PACES

Wander aimlessly around the entire area of the gym until you get winded. Don't forget to act like you own the place/have all the time in the world.

PACE

Whoa, Is that guy in the TapOut shirt grunting at me?

Oh, is my shoe untied?

That smell's not me, right?

MUSCLES USED
- Legs
- Feet
- Back
- Brain (overthinking)

ISOLATED IPOD THUMB CIRCLES

75-100 full circles or until completion of "Getting Brolic" playlist

TOUCH

SHUFFLE

PERFECT!

MUSCLES USED
- Neck
- Wrist
- Thumb
- Back
- Ears
  (jams fully pumped)

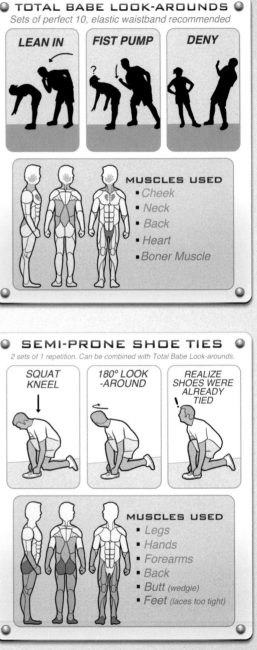

TOTAL BABE LOOK-AROUNDS

Sets of perfect 10, elastic waistband recommended

LEAN IN

FIST PUMP

DENY

MUSCLES USED
- Cheek
- Neck
- Back
- Heart
- Boner Muscle

SEMI-PRONE SHOE TIES

2 sets of 1 repetition. Can be combined with Total Babe Look-arounds.

SQUAT KNEEL

180° LOOK -AROUND

REALIZE SHOES WERE ALREADY TIED

MUSCLES USED
- Legs
- Hands
- Forearms
- Back
- Butt (wedgie)
- Feet (laces too tight)

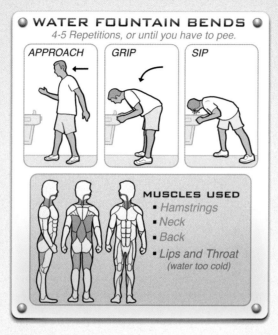

⬤ WATER FOUNTAIN BENDS ⬤

4-5 Repetitions, or until you have to pee.

APPROACH

GRIP

SIP

MUSCLES USED
- *Hamstrings*
- *Neck*
- *Back*
- *Lips and Throat*
  (water too cold)

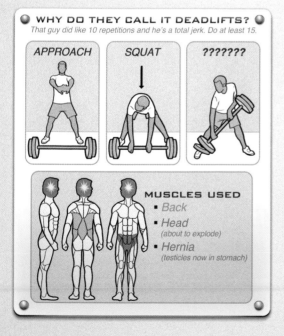

⬤ WHY DO THEY CALL IT DEADLIFTS? ⬤

That guy did like 10 repetitions and he's a total jerk. Do at least 15.

APPROACH

SQUAT

???????

MUSCLES USED
- *Back*
- *Head*
  (about to explode)
- *Hernia*
  (testicles now in stomach)

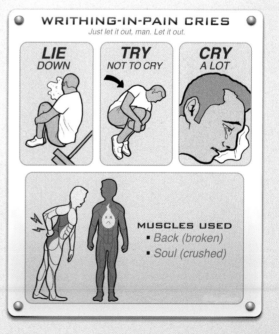

⬤ WRITHING-IN-PAIN CRIES ⬤

Just let it out, man. Let it out.

LIE
DOWN

TRY
NOT TO CRY

CRY
A LOT

MUSCLES USED
- *Back (broken)*
- *Soul (crushed)*

The Honest Older Guy on Your Spring Break Trip

By Steve Hofstetter

Hey, baby! How are you? Good, good, I don't care, good. I only asked because it's easier to see you naked if I seem interested in your thoughts, which are probably about how I have a six pack. Did you notice my six pack?

Where do you go to school? Oh my god! I totally visited there except I didn't! But you don't know that. Hey, what's that bar right by campus that you will say the name of and I'll pretend I knew the name of? Yeah, that one! Do they still have that hot bartender? And they serve that one really cool drink? Don't we seem like friends now? We could totally be friends, if you knew anything true about me and I wasn't a terrible person. Did I show you my six pack?

You and your friends HAVE to come out with us tonight. Because this bar is too bright to roofie you. And I know all the hot spots. That's because I'm 25 and this is the seventh year in a row I've come down here. After I graduated college, I realized that it's hard to meet chicks in the real world. Especially when I work in the mail room of my dad's firm. But that's okay because you think I'm a senior and I'm going to law school next year. And what a coincidence! The law school I said I'm going to go to is like an hour from your campus. You could totally believe we'll ever see each other again.

What do I think about this place? Well, it really is a bit too bright. But I like all the easy girls who convince themselves that I might be the one. As if anyone you meet on vacation when you're drunk and 18 could possibly be the one. Wait, you are 18, right? Whew! I was afraid you might be 19 or 20. You scared me for a minute.

See, you have this romantic notion of what's going to happen down here because movies tell you that love at first sight is possible, maybe even probable. And until now, the closest you've gotten to being in love is a hand job in your prom limo.

I'm here to cash in on that notion. Don't worry; you're not the only one I'm going to take advantage of. There'll be someone else tomorrow. There might even be someone else tonight. Hey, your friend is kind of cute. I might stop making out with you to try to fuck her. But not if you seem easier. I may not be that bright, but I'm not stupid.

SPRING BREAK! I shout that to remind girls that this is a vacation, so their sluttiness doesn't count. I also yell that because I don't know how else to let people know that I am enjoying myself. I DON'T KNOW HOW TO RELATE TO MOST PEOPLE! WOOOOOO!

We should get out of here soon. The longer you and I talk, the sooner you might realize that I'm a pathetic douchebag who can't get girls my own age and spends a few grand each year to have random sex and bury my pain in margaritas. Thankfully, I have extra cash from living with my parents. Man, I'm hoping my dad promotes me soon.

Spring Break?

REALITY = **WORK**

Wrong IM

By Amir Blumenfeld

Soybomb has entered chat

CheezyPoof: Anyway be sure you show up before 6.

Soybomb: Wha?

CheezyPoof: Sorry, Wrong IM

Soybomb: Haha. No Problem ;-)

CheezyPoof: so we talked it over and agreed: zoology is a pseudo-science.

Soybomb: ?

CheezyPoof: Ha! Wrong IM again. Sorry.

Soybomb: that's okay. just remember, i'm Soybomb...

CheezyPoof: I know sorry. my step-cousin's im is kind of like yours.

Soybomb: oh, that's okay. lol. what's his screen name?

CheezyPoof: not that it's any of your fucking business, but it's Sylvester...and then a number (do you REALLY think i'd give you the whole thing)?

Soybomb: okay, my bad. :-/

CheezyPoof: Amir here. And i checked: there's NOTHING illegal about what i'm doing to those "animals." not in THIS country anyway...

Soybomb: woah. i think you've got the wrong im again, amir.

CheezyPoof: ever hear a parrot try and whistle without it's beak?!

Soybomb: I'm signing off.

CheezyPoof: whopsee daiseeee!!! what is WITH me today? i need some vitamin D or something. some Omega 3 for concentration. Question: Are those found in Parrot meat??/?

Soybomb: No idea. Listen.

CheezyPoof: Maybe I should just block you.

Soybomb: Yeah. Exactly what I was gonna sya

Soybomb: *say

CheezyPoof: Kay. I just blocked that dumb zero Patrick Cassels.

Soybomb: Still me.

CheezyPoof HAS SIGNED OFF

CheezyPoof HAS SIGNED ON

CheezyPoof: He's gone. Let's discuss "Phase II: Operation TouCAN'T Sam."

Soybomb: Me again.

CheezyPoof: Is there a pay phone around here?

Soybomb has signed off

124

| New IM | Pictures | Video | Send File ▾ | | Send |

Honest Commencement Program

By Owen Parsons

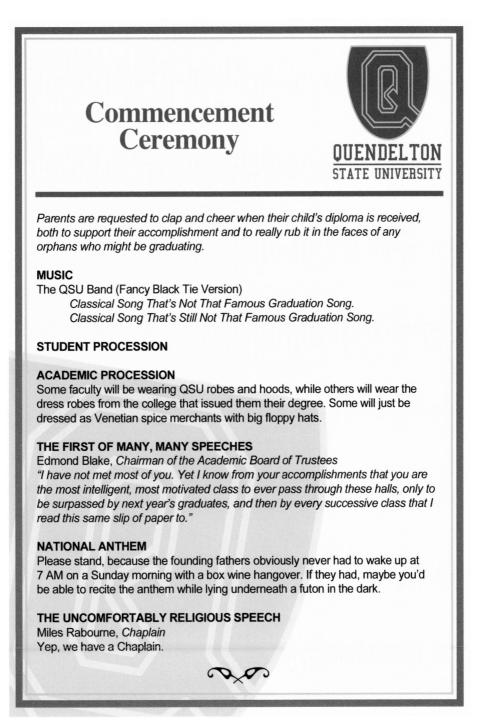

Commencement Ceremony

QUENDELTON STATE UNIVERSITY

Parents are requested to clap and cheer when their child's diploma is received, both to support their accomplishment and to really rub it in the faces of any orphans who might be graduating.

MUSIC
The QSU Band (Fancy Black Tie Version)
> *Classical Song That's Not That Famous Graduation Song.*
> *Classical Song That's Still Not That Famous Graduation Song.*

STUDENT PROCESSION

ACADEMIC PROCESSION
Some faculty will be wearing QSU robes and hoods, while others will wear the dress robes from the college that issued them their degree. Some will just be dressed as Venetian spice merchants with big floppy hats.

THE FIRST OF MANY, MANY SPEECHES
Edmond Blake, *Chairman of the Academic Board of Trustees*
"I have not met most of you. Yet I know from your accomplishments that you are the most intelligent, most motivated class to ever pass through these halls, only to be surpassed by next year's graduates, and then by every successive class that I read this same slip of paper to."

NATIONAL ANTHEM
Please stand, because the founding fathers obviously never had to wake up at 7 AM on a Sunday morning with a box wine hangover. If they had, maybe you'd be able to recite the anthem while lying underneath a futon in the dark.

THE UNCOMFORTABLY RELIGIOUS SPEECH
Miles Rabourne, *Chaplain*
Yep, we have a Chaplain.

125

GREETINGS
Bertram Wright, *President*

ACADEMIC HONORS RECOGNITION
Stanley Glover, *Vice-President*
"...Charles Huang...Lisa Huang...Michael Huang...Rachel Huang..."

INCONSPICUOUS SWIG FROM NALGENE FULL OF "WATER"

GREETINGS AGAIN
Bertram Wright, *President*
"I want to see if I can set the Guinness Record for longest continuous metaphor."

WHOA, WHO ELSE JUST SAW THAT BEACH BALL OVER THERE BY KEVIN?
Kevin rules.

CONFERRAL OF HONORARY DEGREES
Bertram Wright, *President*
"A degree is the highest honor an academic institution can bestow, however in case of emergencies we've got a machine in the Registrar's Office that prints them at like 85¢ a pop."

Recipients
Not Stephen Colbert .... Doctor of Law
Not Stephen Colbert .... Doctor of Science
Minor Celebrity.................... Doctor of Trying To Appease Everyone Who
Signed the Stephen Colbert Petition
Not Stephen Colbert .... Doctor of Law

INTRODUCTION OF THE COMMENCEMENT SPEAKER
Bertram Wright, *President*
"Now I know everyone wanted Stephen Colbert. Stephen Colbert wanted $100,000. I wanted another house to keep my cars in. Guess who got their way?"

COMMENCEMENT ADDRESS
Some Old Guy, *Secretary of Not Being Stephen Colbert*

"Ladies and gentlemen of the Class of 2009. I know most of you are eager to get your diplomas, so I won't bore you. But do pay attention to my...
　　...never had the opportunities that...　　　　　...and then my father said something I'll never...　　　　　...sunscreen...
　　　　　...and all of you will grow up to be President someday."

CONFERRAL OF DOCTORATE DEGREES
Undergraduate students will remain seated for thirty to forty minutes while being upstaged by strangers.

CONFERRAL OF SUDDENLY LESS IMPRESSIVE DEGREES
Names will be read off by fellow classmate Matthew Meyer. Matthew was chosen as a name reader this Spring because of his immense personality and popularity among the graduating class. Matthew will not be joining his classmates in graduating this Spring on account of his heroin charges.

GRADUATION SONG
That's how that tune goes? Then what do I have in my head? Duh-da-duh-da-oh, right, the Duck Tales theme.

HAHA, LOOK AT KEVIN'S SHOES
Classic Kevin.

CLOSING REMARKS
Bertram Wright, President
"See everyone at Applebee's in thirty minutes."

DISMISSAL
Throw those mortarboards up! Yeah!

FIRST POST-COLLEGIATE LESSON: GRAVITY
Ow, hell! They've got corners on them!

ALMA MATER
"Hoorah for Quendelton!"
Composed by a white gentleman who died before good music was invented.

Hoorah! Hoorah! Yippee-yo-hurron!
Something...something Quendelton!
This part used to be racist, but got cleaned up in the Seventies.
This other part's still pretty sexist, though.

Hoorah! Hoorah! Yippee-yo-heree!
Nonsense words are kind of a weak way to write songs.
This line is pretty funny if you substitute in the word "dick."
Seriously, this dude was a songwriter?
How bad was he at everything else?

(chorus) How bad was he at everything else?

Diary of a Charmander

By Brad Einstein

The Cherry Blossom
Brings the Fire Lizard Home
Only in His Dreams

Day 288

Every day is a fresh introduction to Hell.
Trapped in a ball the size of a pomegranate,
forced to fight my way through this pitiful life
by a starry-eyed twelve-year-old. Indeed,
the only time I feel the cool breeze against
my scaly cheek is when I'm engaged in
unwilling combat with something that
looks like a palm tree with legs. Every
day, I pray to a God I am no longer allowed
to believe in for a death that will not come.

I can also hear Squirtle pleasuring himself
in the adjacent Pokeball. It is foul.

— C

Day 312

This afternoon, as I'm scratching haikus into
the wall of my cell (as I'm wont to do), I'm
suddenly caught in a flash of red light. Three
seconds later, I find myself being mauled in
the face by a three-headed ostrich. I try to
reason with him, entreat his sense of justice,
but seeing as we can only say our own names,
it was futile. The one consolation I had
as my skull was being mercilessly crushed into
the ground was that at least when I returned
to my spherical cage, I would not be conscious.

I think today was my birthday.

— C

Day 342

Today I was released from confinement in what
my overlord called a 'PokeCenter! Indeed, every
town we come to has an overcrowded shack where
my bones are hastily set by a woman dressed
like a fetish nurse. As I looked out the window,
I could see the gym towering in the west;
I can't help but to think this entire
infrastructure of oppression is thriving even as
my kidneys fail. Still, I must take time to
count my blessings. For instance, today I
was actually given something to drink; it
was delicious. The momentary joy of tasting
water was soon brought to an end, however,
as I soon discovered I've become deaf
in one ear.

I should be upset, but in a world such
as mine, what music is there to hear?

128 — C

Day 368

Today, my stomach started curdling at the sight of my electric nemesis—Pikachu. I cannot comprehend how that yellow rat may walk beneath the sky whilst I am held captive in a bi-colored tennis ball. He may see the rising of the moon and feel the changing of the seasons, while I am trapped within the obsidian core of this tiny, insufferable globe, forced to sit in a pool of my own filth. That static-charged Judas has gained favor with our prepubescent tyrant by turning a blind eye to the enslavement of his people, and he will someday pay for these sins. Someday, my anguished bellows will echo in his ears as the light slowly fades from his adorably oversized eyes.

As a side note, I can no longer hear the sound of my mother's voice.

-C

Day 407

It has been a fortnight since I have last seen the sun. An infection seems to have grappled hold of my lungs and renders me useless for even the most menial of tasks. There was once a time where I knew I could at least count on being momentarily freed to start a fire, solve a puzzle, or reheat a meal my master would never dream of sharing, but now, it isn't so. Whene're I attempt to summon fire from my belly, naught is produced but a pile of clotted lung-blood and soot. I can feel my time drawing nigh, and though I have known only misery and fear at the hands of the human child, I do not begrudge my fate.

On second thought, Yes. Yes I do.

-C

129

Chest Hair Cycle

By Caldwell Tanner

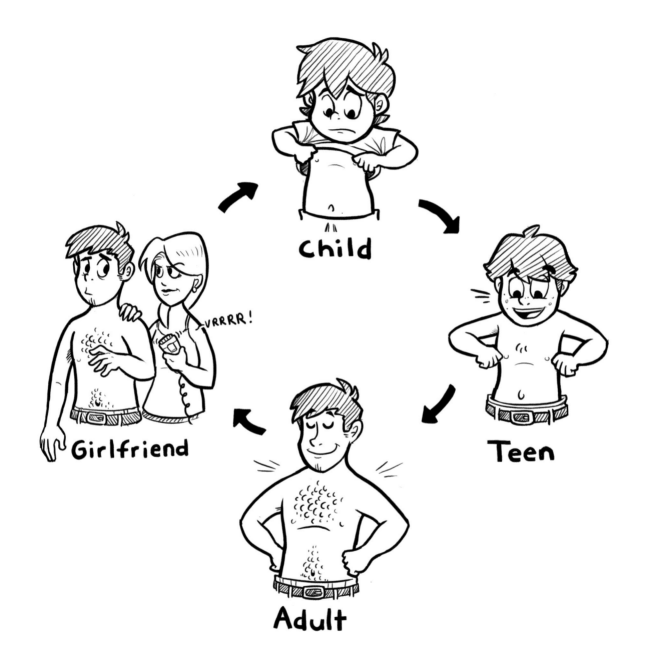

Questionable Excerpts from My Poorly Edited Autobiography

By Patrick Cassels

p. 37

Beads of sweat flew from my forearm as I swung my machete through the tangled thicket of rubber-tree plants and bamboo. "Onward, men!" I cried in a voice still raw from shouting plays to my fellow Pittsburg Steelers during the previous week's playoffs against the Raiders. "Onward, I say! We must get this treasure to the troops before sundown, or Baghdad is as good as lost!"

p. 151

It's true that I was under the influence of LSD for the better part of 1967. But when I regained consciousness, the Beatles had released Sgt. Pepper's Lonely Hearts Club Band. Am I saying I wrote this legendary record? Of course not—music that timeless practically writes itself.

p. 400

An angioplasty is a difficult surgery to perform under any condition, let alone while navigating a Mercedes along the unpaved roads of Prague. Fortunately, Angelina's extensive humanitarian work had made her a surprisingly capable nurse. With a little luck, I was certain Jodie Foster would be healthy enough to do three-way sex by the time we reached Switzerland.

p. 890

They say you never forget the face of the first man you kill. This is especially true when that man is Adolf Hitler.

p. 1503

Standing atop a hill of skulls 20 feet high, I pointed my iron broadsword above my head as a bolt of lightning shot across the orange sky. "You've won!" cried the Princess with a smile. She grazed her hand across my bare, sweat-coated chest, causing a commotion beneath my griffin-skin loin cloth to rival that of the thunder that crashed above us. I flipped my ponytail back and chuckled. "What the fuck is victory in this fucking fucked up world?" Then I put on my sunglasses and frenched her for 45 minutes.

At least the children were safe.

THE END

(OR IS IT…?)

Where I Hide My Porn

By Jeff Rosenberg

Desktop

- Desktop
  - My Documents
    - Adobe
    - AdobeStockPhotos
    - AIMLogger
    - Corel User Files
    - Cute College Girl
    - Cyberlink
    - Downloads
    - Filelib
    - My eBooks
    - My Games
    - My Google Gadgets
    - My Music
    - My Pix
    - My PSP Files
    - My Videos
    - My Widgets
    - Picture Package
    - Random Stuff
      - Facebook Profile Pics
      - Family Stuff
        - Cape Cod
        - the grand canyon
        - uncle floyd and aunt beth's 50th
          - Aunt Floyd Anniversary Pix
            - New Folder
              - New Folder
                - Error 1325531-G
                  - Missing Files
                    - Infected
                      - 100110101
                        - MOOOVIES
                          - Asian
                          - black
                          - white
                          - horses
        - Cousin Sal the Diabetic
          - Vampire Porn
        - Dad Dancing
        - Event Pictures
      - Vacations
    - Me and Lisa
    - Stegosaurus
  - Schoolwork
  - My Computer
  - My Network Places
  - Recycle Bin

132

The Future of Warfare

By Streeter Seidell

Ypres, Belgium - November 15, 1914

The Battle of Ypres rages as two German soldiers keep watch over the British trenches.

Soldier 1 My God, who would have thought soldiers would be reduced to this? Sitting in trenches, firing these machine guns at each other. There is little honor to be had here.

Soldier 2 Yes, yes. But one must never forget we serve a higher purpose than ourselves: the great German fatherland. If I die for Germany, I die with honor.

Soldier 1 Indeed, but if I must die for Germany, let it be by the blade, not some unseen bullet or bomb.

Soldier 2 We are fighting a different war than in times past, my friend. A modern war. World War I will be looked on as a turning point for military technology and deployment.

Soldier 1 I cou— Now wait a minute, what did you call this war?

Soldier 2 ...What did I say?

Soldier 1 I believe you called this "World War I."

Soldier 2 Did I? I meant to say; 'The Great War,' 'of course.

Soldier 1 Ah, yes. I thought you a fortune-telling gypsy for a second!

Soldier 2 If you were not my closest friend, I would have your ear for such a comment!

Soldier 1 Merely a joke, friend. World War I? Ha! As if anyone knows the future! Besides, this is the war to end allwars. The Great War!

Soldier 2 The Greatest of Wars, so far!

Soldier 1 Agr— Again, "so far?" Have you some plan, my friend?

Soldier 2 A plan? Ha! What use is planning in uncertain times? If I live through World War I, I will most likely return to my passion: pai—

Soldier 1 There! You did it again! You called it—

A Lieutenant approaches the soldiers' position.

Lieutenant Private Hitler, grab your weapon and report to command.

Soldier 2 Well, it appears as if I'm needed.

Soldier 1 Godspeed, friend. Do Germany proud!

Soldier 2 My friend, I would never do anything to shame the Fatherland! To arms!

College Girl's Diary, as Imagined by Me

By Jeff Rosenberg

March 19, 2008

Dear Diary,

Ugh, I hate school so much. Classes blow and my roommates suck. Plus all the boys at this school are complete tool douches. Well, all except one boy. He's really shy so he's never come up to talk to me, but he's just so adorable and not like the other boys. He doesn't have to impress anyone, ya know? He gets by on wearing beat-up sweatpants to class and a worn out Chicago Bulls tee with huge grease stains in the middle. Sometimes he wears this really dirty high school hoodie and uses his sleeve as a tissue, but every time I see him it's like a slip n slide down there.

—Wet

March 25, 2008

Dear Diary,

I hate that I have to act like such a phony all the time. It's my stupid friends and their narrow minded sororstitute mentality. They're always judging people on like, how hairless their North Face is or something stupid like that. I just wish I wasn't such a wuss and could just go up to Jeff. I know he's kind of weird but I think that's way hot. I mean, yeah I saw him stuffing chicken nuggets from the dining hall into his pockets and pumping ketchup into a Ziploc bag right before eating a meal entirely made up of oatmeal cookies and Hi-C, but I love quirky guys! They always have something fun and interesting to say which makes me horny.

— Horny like a bull!

March 25, 2008

Dear Diary,

I skipped all my classes today just so I could masturbate to this boy. I masturbated like 15 times to Jeff and maybe once to Uncle Jessie from Full House in between, but that's just because I wanted to give Jeff a break. After that I was beat so I just sat in my room in a black thong and watched re-runs of Boy Meets World on ABC Family as I ate spoonful after spoonful of chunky peanut butter. Today was so funny! Jeff ate cold General Tso's chicken in class with his bare hands then wiped the sauce off in the inside of the pouch of that hoodie. I think he was really hung over too, which is off because it was Tuesday and we were in the middle of taking the midterm.

— I'm moist like a kitchen sponge

March 29, 2008

Dear Diary,

Got smashed Friday night and fingered myself in the bathroom stall again. Ain't no thang though. Hahah no it's cool. I just ate an entire bag of Doritos though. Cooler Ranch. After I popped myself. Sometimes I see Jeff staring at me in my peripheral, but when I try to catch him he just closes his eyes and slowly turns his head back. Today I saw him on campus taking a nap on the quad. He was spooning his Dell Inspiron 9300 while clutching an empty Jolt energy drink and half empty bottle of Quaaludes, which my mom told me are a really strong sedative that were popular in the 70's. It took every morsel of my will power not to jump on him right there and profess my unrequited love.

— Dripping like a leaky faucet!

March 30, 2008

Dear Diarrhea,

I think I'm in love. Any man that can do that many tricks with a yo-yo must be a demigod in bed! He's just not afraid to express himself, like yesterday when he was organizing his Magic the Gathering cards during our Calc midterm. He just doesn't give a damn and that's what I need in my life. I can only hope our paths cross by some fateful event and he falls madly in love with me forever. I'm getting light headed just thinking about us together and I think I'm building up the courage to talk to him this week... if he ever wakes up from his barbiturate-induced coma.

Heading to the shower to pump some flow on the bean!

Jessica!

A Kid Whose Parents Just Got Divorced Writes a Book

By Brian Murphy

Somtims mommys and daddys can live in other houses and still love eachoher.

My mommy loves my dad so much she cries caus she misses him! What a baby

Daddy is more fun hes not a baby. He drives a cool car and we have slepovers on weekends. Fun!

Sometims dad has his frend over. Thats when I have fun becus they go in his room and I can do whatever I want. I can even eat candy!

Mommy is mean and dosnt like daddys frend. I think you shood always be nice to new frends. Mom says her name is Bich.

Somtimes I can hear Daddy and Bich wrestling I can tell hes winning because of the sounds she makes.

That is how love works.

Bowser's Suggestion Box

By Streeter Seidell

NAME:
Boo

SUGGESTION:
Come ON! It's RETARDED that we can only get him when he's not looking! RETARDED!

NAME:
CHAIN CHOMP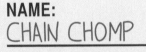

SUGGESTION:
Some of us would be better if we didn't have to be on chains cuz then he couldn't jump over us

NAME:
Larry Koopa

SUGGESTION:
Maybe the kingdom would be safer without all the wharp whistles you hid? Just saying.

NAME:
Hammer Bros.

SUGGESTION:
We should be able to throw hammers right at him because since we have to lob them we don't get him as much as we could.

NAME:
Mouser

SUGGESTION:
I feel like some of us aren't being used that often.

NAME:
BULLET BILL

SUGGESTION:
WHY COME WE BAD FOR HIM IF JUMP UP BUT NO IF HE JUMP DOWN?

NAME:
Koopa Troopa

SUGGESTION:
I know you said he would never find all the stuff (mushrooms, stars, etc.) that you hid in the ? boxes but he totally does. Why even put that stuff anywhere at all?

139

Promised Land

By Lev Novak

God Hey, so Moses, sorry about the forty years of wandering. That was maybe six years over the line.

Moses But not the slavery, huh?

God Eh.

Moses Okay. Well, at least it's worth it, right? Why, a land flowing with milk and honey—

God Yeah, um, its just sand.

Moses Excuse me?

God Turns out it's just burning, awful sand. Seriously. I don't even know why I said all that other stuff.

Moses Oh.

God And you're going to have to fight all the Canaanites for it. There is going to be a lot of dying. Man, I totally forgot about those guys…

Moses Could we…just have different sand then?

God No. This is holy land for you, the Muslims and Christians.

Moses Wait, who?

God Oh right…yeah, I may have promised this land a bunch…

Moses You overbooked Israel. Great.

God Sorry, Mo. I'm not a math person.

Moses Do you literally not know of any other lands to assign?

God …Or a geography person. Or a person, really.

Moses So how are we going to solve this?

God I dunno. I guess we're going to have to see who wants it more, you know?

Moses So—

God Fight! Fight! Fight!

Moses Couldn't we just share this…awful, awful sand?

God No! What part of "this is your holy land alone, and also their holy land alone, and it's just for you or for them, but I'm also everywhere" is confusing?

Moses All of that. All of that is confusing.

God Well whatever. Just fight over your promised land which is also other people's promised land, okay? I'm totally rooting for you. Or them. Huh. It's pretty unclear…

Moses Yeah.

God I can only hope people will explain my intentions by yelling things.

MapQuest Helps You Find the Clitoris

By Dan Gurewitch

Total Est. Time: 11 minutes, 42 seconds   **Total Est. Distance:** 84 miles, 3.2 bases

Advanced Options:

[X] Shortest Route   [ ] Shortest Time (Less Lubricated)
[ ] Avoid Tolls   [ ] Avoid Foreplay
[ ] Avoid Humiliation

↓	1. Start out going **SOUTH** on the **NECK** toward **CLEAVAGE**.	2.1 inches
↻	2. Follow the **ROUNDABOUT** around the **LEFT BREAST**.	5.4 inches
EXIT ⬅	3. Take the 2nd exit toward **RIGHT BREAST / SIDEBOOB / ARMPIT**.	3.1 inches
↻	4. Follow the **ROUNDABOUT** around the **RIGHT BREAST**.	5.4 inches
↓	5. **RIGHT BREAST** becomes **TORSO**.	.3 inches
EXIT ⬅	6. Merge onto **HAIRWAY TO HEAVEN SOUTH** via exit 14B on the **LEFT** toward **BELLY BUTTON** (Portions toll).	10.5 inches
↓	7. Continue to follow **HAIRWAY TO HEAVEN SOUTH** (crossing into **MONS PUBIS**).	2.2 inches
EXIT	8. Take the **VULVA** exit – exit 19 – toward **LABIA MAJORA / LABIA MINORA / ANUS**.	.1 inches
EAST 90	9. Keep **RIGHT** to take **I-90 E / MASSACHUSETTS TURNPIKE** toward **N.H.-MAINE / BOSTON**.	84 miles
➡	10. Turn **RIGHT**.	<.1 inches
⬅	11. Turn **LEFT**.	<.1 inches
➡	12. Turn **RIGHT**.	<.1 inches
⬅	13. Turn **LEFT**.	<.1 inches
✳	14. End at **ANUS**.	
SORRY	15. **APOLOGIZE**.	.2 minutes
➡	16. Turn **RIGHT**.	<.1 inches
➡	17. Turn **RIGHT** to follow **VULVA NORTH** toward **CLITORIS**.	1.6 inches
⬭	18. End at **CLITOR -**	
⬅	19. Turn **LEFT**.	<.1 inches
➡	20. Turn **RIGHT**.	<.1 inches
⬅	21. Turn **LEFT**.	<.1 inches
⬭	22. End at **CLITORIS, VUL -**	
⬅	23. Turn **LEFT**.	<.1 inches
➡	24. Turn **RIGHT**.	<.1 inches
END	25. End at **CLITORIS, VULVA, US**.	

By Jason Michaels

143

JK Rowling's Deleted Harry Potter Character

By Owen Parsons and Ben Joseph

An early manuscript of the Harry Potter saga recently revealed the many revisions the novels went through before publication. Of the changes, most notable is a fourth main character, Kenny Nesbit, completely absent from the final draft.

Chapter 7 – The Obvious Answer

Kenny and Harry both stood silently in front of the headmaster's desk. Dumbledore's eyes glittered, but Harry sensed there was a deeper sense of concern hiding just beyond his gaze.

"Harry," Dumbledore said, stroking his long white beard, "your godfather, Sirius Black, has escaped from Azkaban Prison."

Harry gaped. "The man who killed my parents? But...but that's..." He tried to say more, but his mouth had gone dry. No words came.

Dumbledore rested his hands together and leaned forward over his desk, locking his wise old eyes with Harry's. "I assure you, Harry, we can confirm that he's nowhere near Hogwarts. We've searched the entire area, except for the spooky old haunted house that no one goes into, ever, for any reason."

Kenny raised his hand. "So let's assume, for a minute, that the murderer who doesn't want to be found is hiding in the one place no one would ever look. Why don't we take one quick peek in the haunted house, and if he is in there, *which he definitely is*, we can arrest him and get rid of those horrible soul-eating demons you let loose in the school to look for him."

Dumbledore frowned. "Kenny, the situation you describe is impossible. I just explained that no one goes in that house. It's very spooky and we're scared of it."

"It wouldn't make sense," agreed Harry. At that very moment, a horrible, nearly headless ghost drifted through the room. Harry and Dumbledore waved to it politely.

"Nothing here makes any fucking sense," Kenny muttered to himself.

Chapter 37 – The Lunchtime Quandary

Harry sighed loudly. Kenny cursed under his breath and ignored him, staring intently into his pudding cup. Harry sighed again, louder this time.

"What's wrong, Harry?" Hermione asked. Kenny groaned.

"Oh, it's nothing," Harry said. "It's just that all the Slytherin Quidditch players have got the latest Nimbus 2001 broomsticks. There's no way we can beat them riding our older brooms."

Kenny dropped his pudding spoon. "WHAT? Dude, we're wizards. We have a spell that creates birds. Live. Freaking. Birds. Ignoring the horrifying implications of creating life from the void for a second, can't you just summon a few extra shekels and go buy some better brooms?"

"Because, Kenny," Hermione said, smirking, "Magic can't make money. The Principal Exceptions to Gamp's Law..."

"Holy crap, woman," Kenny interrupted. "We get it. You read books." He turned back to Harry. "Look, dude, we've all got our own problems. We can' drop everything and listen to you whine because the rich kids have better sports equipment than you."

"But it's the championship game!" Harry cried.

"Hey, why don't you *accio* someone who gives a shit. Or better yet, here: *accio awesome broomsticks!*"

Seven sleek racing broomsticks flew into the middle of the hallway and fell to the ground with a loud clatter.

"Look at that," Kenny said. "Why do we even have money? Why is there a wizard economy, or even society, if everybody can just wave a stick and get WHATEVER MATERIAL POSSESSIONS THEY WANT? DID ANYBODY THINK THIS UNIVERSE THROUGH?"

Chapter 19 – The Very Short Quidditch Match

Harry Potter darted through the sky, dodging Slytherin blockers left and right. If he could only catch the golden snitch, then—

"I GOT IT!"

Harry whipped his head around. There was Kenny Nesbit, clutching the tiny golden snitch in his hands. Oliver Wood, the Gryffindor team captain, flew angrily towards Kenny.

"Kenny! What are you doing? You're a chaser. Your job is to throw the quaffle through the hoop!"

"Oh, you mean the ball that scores ten points? Yeah, I made the executive decision to de-prioritize that in favor of grabbing the little gold ball that WINS THE WHOLE FREAKIN' GAME. BOO-YAH!" Kenny pumped his fist in the air and made a rather suggestive motion toward several attractive witches in the crowd.

"But..." Harry Potter sniffled. "I'm the seeker. It's my job to catch the snitch."

Kenny rolled his eyes. "There's no 'Potter' in 'team,' okay?" He turned to the team. "Listen up, guys. From now on, everyone's a Seeker, regardless of whether your parents are dead or not."

At the mention of his parents, tears welled up in Harry's eyes. The rest of the team glared at Kenny as if he was a pile of house goblin excrement.

"Hey, sorry," Kenny quickly backtracked, "That parent crack wasn't directed at anyone in particular. Delwood's dad is dead, too."

"My dad's in Azkaban!" Delwood cried.

"Whatever. If no one's going to recognize how great I am at this retarded sport, then I quit. Witches prefer rule-breaking bad boys, anyway. Right, Hermione?"

In the stands, Hermione shifted uncomfortably in her seat.

Chapter 14 – The New Professor

"I wonder who our next Defense Against the Dark Arts professor will be?"

Kenny spat out his Butterbeer across the table, drenching Ron.

"Hey!" Ron cried.

"Shut up," Kenny said. He turned to Harry. "Harry, are you still taking that class? Everyone who teaches it has secretly been a crazy person who later tried to kill you."

Harry thought about it for a moment. "That may be, but we have to learn more about the dark arts if we're going to stand a chance against Voldemort!"

"You know what else would help you stand a chance against Voldemort? Not being dead. Maybe you should take a class in that. If you want to get crazy, you could even take it at a school where there aren't ogres, basilisks, and crazy murdering teachers. Sup Draco."

Kenny leaned out and delivered a high-five to the blonde Slytherin as he passed. He turned back just in time to see Harry being attacked by a giant, razor-winged iguana spider.

"Look, Kenny!" Harry laughed, as shrieking mandibles dripped venom inches from his face. "Look what Hagrid found! Isn't it delightful?"

Kenny threw up his hands. "Screw this. I'm going up on the roof to smoke. Anyone else want to join me?"

"I will," said Hermione immediately. Ron looked glumly at the ground, saying nothing.

Chapter 29 – The Shocking Development

Harry surveyed the assembled members of Dumbledore's Army. He hoped the motley group of young wizards were up to the dark task ahead.

"To beat Voldemort," Harry announced, "We must find his seven horcruxes. They could be anything and anywhere—"

"Whoa, hold up." Kenny Nesbit said. Harry had balked at the idea of including Kenny in the Army, but Hermione, for some reason, had insisted. "Six years of fighting this guy and we end up on a quest for seven arbitrary items? Did Voldemort play a lot of Japanese RPGs as a kid?"

Ron put his hand on Kenny's shoulder. "Voldemort's got to be stopped, Kenny. He's pure evil."

"Right, so why are we just hearing about horcruxes? Didn't anyone think to look this up before now? Jesus, this is dumber than the Room of Requirement."

"You mean the room that appears only when needed," Harry said, "and then transforms into whatever we need it to be?"

"Do you even hear how stupid that sounds? Okay, new plan: instead of going on a scavenger hunt, I'm going to go tell the British Army about this new terrorist guy named Voldemort. Let's see him hex his way out of a carpet bombing."

With that, Kenny marched out of the meeting. He paused briefly at the door.

"Also, I'm definitely banging Hermione. Sorry, Weasley."

The Mother from Hush Little Baby Makes Some Returns

By Dan Gurewitch

Hi. I hate to be a bother, but yesterday I purchased this long-tailed mockingbird, and it wasn't quite what I expected. No, it doesn't sing at all. So, if it's not too much of a hassle, I guess I'll make an even exchange for the next best thing – this 4-karat diamond ring. Oh, yes, I can pay the additional $52,400. He's a very picky baby.

So I bought this diamond ring yesterday afternoon, and gave it to my baby. It's none of your business "why." The point is that when I woke up this morning, it was brass. How does that even happen? I didn't pay $52,400 for my diamond to go reverse Rumpelstiltskin. You know what? Just give me a looking glass. My baby is not going to be happy about this.

Okay, hi. The looking glass broke. I think what did it was my baby's high-pitched agonized scream when he realized he was getting a mirror instead of that 4-karat diamond. Do babies even like anything other than mockingbirds and diamonds? You know what, fine. Just get me a Billy Goat from the Goat aisle. No, I don't need any gruff with that. Jesus Christ.

I have a question. What use does my baby have for a Billy Goat that won't pull? Obviously you have not met my baby. My baby has a large collection of heavy metal objects, and he needs them continuously relocated. You think he can do it himself? He's a Goddamn baby! Look, just let me exchange the goat for this cart and bull. My baby has goods to be transported, and he doesn't have all day.

Well, I'm glad I kept the receipt. That cart and bull hadn't even made one full trip when it turned right over. Shoddy alignment. You can imagine how my baby felt, seeing his large collection of copper flow check valves and stainless steel tubing tumble into the mud. Can I just get a dog instead? Listen carefully: it needs to be a dog that is already named Rover, prior to my purchase. Yes, I'm serious – my baby knows what he likes and he does not fuck around.

Just shut up and get me your supervisor. Why? Because the dog won't bark. Did you raise him with the mockingbird? Do you only sell mute animals? Does anything in this fucking store work? Shut your mouth! I'm running out of options here. I expect no trouble exchanging this dog, logically, for a horse and cart. This is your last chance to restore my baby's faith in commercial trade!

Hello. Look, I was going to storm in here and yell at you about the horse and cart (which fell down, what a surprise!), but that's not important now. I bought a cradle from you a few months ago, and you told me it was treetop-safe. Well guess what, the wind blew, the cradle rocked, the bough broke, and down came the baby, cradle and all. Long story short: he died. So I won't be making any more exchanges.

Also, do you know where the nearest Salvation Army is? I have like twelve onesies that I don't need any more.

If Websites Were Pets

By Caldwell Tanner

FACEBOOK

Kind of annoying, and caring for it takes up more of your time than you'd like to admit.

YOUTUBE

Fun to watch, and very good at wasting your time.

MYSPACE

You haven't checked on it in years, how is it still alive?

4CHAN

*Slightly amusing,
but also kinda gross*

REDTUBE

Whoa, I'm pretty sure that thing
will give you a ton of viruses if
you're not careful, dude.

GOOGLE

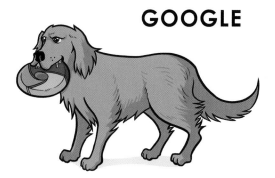

*Reliable, and not likely to abandon
you anytime soon (you hope).*

BING

Good at playing fetch, but maybe
not as good as your other dog.

The Imagination Of Wendell Blatt As He Goes Trick or Treating

By Jake Hurwitz and Streeter Seidell

Cynthia Hey look at Wendell walking down the street alone, he's so brave.

Stephanie And smart, there's no one to slow him down. He's getting maximum candy.

Cynthia Look at how he eats his candy and litters the wrappers as he goes. He doesn't follow any rules!

Across the street, Wendell rings a doorbell. A man answers.

Man Ah! You scared me, with your costume. Not the way you smell. Like milk.

Wendell Trick or treat.

Man You are not too old for this at all. Good move carrying two pillow cases by the way, let me give you some more candy for those.

Stephanie He's cleaning up! And look at that costume, it's so retro and original. A ghost.

Cynthia Did you see all the semen stains on his bed sheet? He must get laid all the time.

Stephanie I know I'd bone him.

Cynthia Ditto. I just had an orgasm thinking about it.

Stephanie We should show him our boobs sometime.

Randy Why do you guys like Wendell? He doesn't have any friends. He's not even invited to my Halloween party tonight.

Cynthia Maybe he didn't wanna come 'cause your party is gay and I don't wanna go out with you anymore.

Randy Fair enough. I'm so stupid and I don't even own a bow staff, while Wendell has 3.

Wendell rings another doorbell. An old woman answers.

Woman Wow, this is your third time coming to my house. And I respect your persistence! Here's the King Size candy bar I've been hiding.

Stephanie That was so impressive.

Randy Did you guys know I have a vagina?

Wendell goes to ring a doorbell but sees a bowl of candy with a note by the door.

Note Please take one, unless you're Wendell Blatt in which case the whole bucket is yours. And you only get bad grades in math 'cause the teacher is dumb, not you.

Cynthia Whoa, is that Wendell's mom talking to those high school boys down the street?

Stephanie Don't worry, there's gotta be a good reason.

Down the street.

Mrs. Blatt So long story short, you guys can't come over anymore, Wendell's dad is moving back in.

High School Boy

We will never come to the house again.

Mrs. Blatt   And Mr. Blatt is getting a new used Daewoo and it's super fast and awesome and Wendell can ride in the front seat.

High School Boy

Daewoo's are great cars. Sure they're inexpensive, but they're well made. What's wrong with a bargain?

Mrs. Blatt   Yes, nothing is wrong with a good bargain. Remember, don't come to the house anymore.

High School Boy

Never again.

153

What You're Saying with Your Hand-Raising Style

By Susanna Wolff

The Ooh Ooh, I Know!

ME! I KNOW! Look at the way I'm supporting my outstretched arm with my other arm! If you don't call on me, I might die. At the very least I'm going to start whimpering. WHY ARE YOU NOT CALLING ON ME?! I'm in the front row and I've been holding my arm up for so long that it's starting to shake. LOOK AT ME! I can't feel my fingers anymore. I also don't remember what I'm raising my hand to say, BUT PLEASE CALL ON ME ANYWAY OR I'M GOING TO HAVE TO START BOUNCING IN MY SEAT!!!

The Nonchalant

Uh, yeah, I might have something to say. Not a big deal though. You can call on me. Or not. Whatever. I don't really know why I want to answer your question. It's not like I care. Hold on, I got a text message. I'm going to read that and then you can call on me if you feel like it. But don't worry, I'm going to keep the phone level with my thigh while I text so it looks like I respect this class even though we all know that I don't. I should probably put my phone on silent.

The Back Row

I've been watching the Sopranos illegally online all class, but I reached my 72 minute limit on Megavideo, so I decided to Wikipedia what you're talking about. Now I'm going to ask a really specific question so you think I did the reading and that hot girl 3 seats down thinks I'm one of those genius slackers that only really exist in teen dramadies. I love disproving stereotypes about people who sit in the back row. Oh, sweet. Friday Night Lights is on Netflix Instant Play.

The Note-Taker

Oh man, I wish I could raise my hand and answer your question, but I am just so busy taking notes. I obviously know the answer, but I mean, you understand. I have to keep writing the word "Hemoglobin" over and over again until you're convinced that I'm busy, yet studiously attentive, and you call on someone else. Why do I only take notes when you're asking questions? Ah, let me write that question down and vigorously avoid eye contact. I think that kid who's bouncing in his seat knows though.

The One Finger Dissent

Uh, I'm going to have to disagree actually. I know you haven't finished talking, but I can already tell that I disagree. I'm pretty sure the professor disagrees too. I mean, psh, I can see that she's nodding and smiling at you, but she and I have a more subtle understanding. Right, professor? Professor?

The Maybe

Yeah, what I was going to say is that I like to start my comments with "I was going to say" and then proceed to say what I was going to say, thus making that phrasing illogical. So, um, I think you might want to call on me? Also, I'll make my last sentence sound like a question because I'm not confident about what I'm saying?

The Hands Free

I'M TALKING. LISTEN TO ME TALK. JUST TRY TO GET ME TO STOP TALKING. I DON'T CARE THAT CLASS ENDS IN 30 SECONDS. I'M GOING TO ASK A COMPLICATED QUESTION AND NOD ATTENTIVELY WHILE THE PROFESSOR ANSWERS. THE FACT THAT EVERYONE IN THE ROOM WANTS TO PUNCH ME IN THE NECK DOES NOT MATTER. ALL THAT MATTERS IS THAT I AM TALKING RIGHT NOW AND YOU ARE NOT.

Hardware Store Employee Manual

By Streeter Seidell

PART 3 AVOIDING CUSTOMERS

Though management has gone to great lengths to avoid it, customers will often attempt to extract information from you regarding where products are within the store. This is generally a waste of your time. Refer to the guide for help to better avoid customers.

METHOD 1 HIDING

Each store has been strategically laid out to provide ample hiding space for employees. See chart for examples.

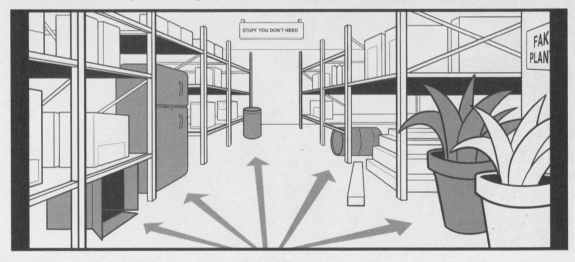

DISGUISE

Should a hiding spot not be readily available, try to conceal the fact that you are employed by us by cloaking yourself in a jacket. Your apron concealed, it should be easier to blend in with the customers.

DENY AND RE-ROUTE

Should methods 1 and 2 prove insufficient, the next tactic attempted should be method 3: Deny and Re-Route. Granted, this will require some customer interaction, but it is designed to minimize and conclude such distractions as quickly as possible. Simply follow the steps below.

THE PUSH AND PLAY

METHOD 4

Should all 3 of the above tactics fail, you may find that you need to resort to the Push and Play. This method, by far the most labor intensive, should only be deployed in times of dire customer overload, such as any summer holiday weekend.

A Find a heavy piece of something or other and put it on a cart.

B Place iPod earbuds in ear.

C Push and Play

'cuse me! 'cuse me! ...Concrete jungle where dreams are made of... 'cuse me!

NOBODY SHOULD BOTHER YOU NOW!

Avoiding our customers is a cornerstone of our business and we rely on each employee to take it upon him or herself to make sure not a single customer finds help in our stores easy to come by. Helping customers takes valuable time away from our main work objective: smoking cigarettes behind the pallets of stone out back!

Meat Loaf Reveals What He Won't Do for Love

By Brian Murphy

Meat Loaf	You like it when The Loaf kisses your neck?
Girl	Ohhhh yeah, baby. Just like th— Wait!
Meat Loaf	What's wrong?
Girl	You can't just get right to it like that.
Meat Loaf	Why not?
Girl	We need...you know. Foreplay.
Meat Loaf	Oh. Wow. Yeah. Not really my thing.
Girl	I thought you said you'd do anything for love?
Meat Loaf	Right. But I won't do that.
Girl	That's what you were talking about? I always thought it was something more profound...
Meat Loaf	Nope. I just don't like going down on chicks.
Girl	So you'd go to "hell and back" before you'd perform oral sex on me?
Meat Loaf	Haha, now you're just trying to make me sound bad.
Girl	I just don't think it's fair.
Meat Loaf	Look, The Loaf doesn't need foreplay to get chicks wet.

Meat Loaf summons a demon band and plays a 10-minute epic power ballad that turns the sky black, causes earthquakes, and opens a portal to Hell. Every woman on Earth orgasms twice.

Girl	I'm so...satisfied...I think I might die.
Meat Loaf	They always do.

Meat Loaf rides off to Hell on a motorcycle

160

How the Movie Rating System Actually Works

By Jeff Rubin

G — GOD, WHY DID I HAVE KIDS?

Movies for babies, bored parents, stoners and weirdos who love cartoons. These films contain nothing interesting. Even most Pixar movies are PG.

PG — POOP GAGS

Contains family-friendly material kids aged 12-19 may find "lame."

PG-13 — SAME AS PG BUT, YOU KNOW,13-IER

You can still show PG-13 movies on cable without editing them, making this a completely meaningless designation. Probably more violence than sex.

R — RADICAL FUCKING MOVIE

Movies for cool kids 12 and over, or anybody 15 and over. If you can't handle an R-rated movie by the time you're 15, you're probably going to go crazy anyway. Terrible parents with crying babies may also be admitted.

NC-17 — NOBODY C'S THESE MOVIES

NC-17 films may contain excessive violence and graphic nudity, yet somehow they're still boring. Theaters may only admit very mature individuals, such as 17-year-olds.

If Moms Wrote Science Textbooks

By Sarah Schneider

◁▯▢ SCIENCE FUNDAMENTALS 1.1

The Carpenter Theory of Layering

First discovered by Joan Carpenter of Missoula, Montana, the Carpenter Theory of Layering states that no person is capable of accurately determining how many layers they will require when going outside.

This phenomenon holds true regardless of age, temperature or the fact that you've already been outside once today. To explain the relationship between variables at work, Carpenter developed a formula.

Carpenter's Formula:

$$(Lt) + 2 = X$$

Where L is the number of layers one thinks he or she will need at any given temperature (t) and X is the actual number of layers required.
For instance, let's say t=32 degrees, which dictates an L value of 3. Using Carpenter's Formula, we see that the true number of layers required is actually 5, and you can thank her later.

If one were to go outside with any fewer than Carpenter's number of layers, one would immediately develop the flu.

◁▯▢ SCIENCE FUNDAMENTALS 1.2

The First Law of Germ Conductivity

The First Law of Germ Conducivity was discovered by Martha Middleton of Summit, New Jersey and is based upon Nancy Oppenhauer's Germ Theory, which states that germs are literally everywhere at all times.

The First Law of Conducivity states that those germs living in the air can only be conducted to the epidermis by wet hair.

Fig 1. Germs bounce off dry hair, as the arid strands make conduction impossible

Fig. 2 Wet hair, on the contrary creates a series of lubricated pathways that allow the germs to reach the epidermis easily.
Fig 3. Once the epidermis has been breached, the germs go everywhere.

Editor's Note: Martha Middleton has insisted that her Second through Fifteenth Laws of Conductivity are of equal importance to her First Law, but authorities have denied these claims considering that they are just the First Law over and over again.

Fig 1.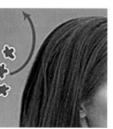

Fig 2.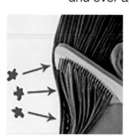

Fig 3.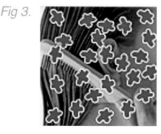

Caterman's Rule of Blindness

First postulated in 1963, immediately following the invention of television. Cheryl Caterman's Rule of Blindness was the first to directly link sitting too close to the television with blindness.

(Many experts use Caterman's Rule of Blindness in conjunction with Caterman's Rule of Frying Your Brain.)

Caterman's Formula of Blindness

$$(D \times H) \times PO = X$$

D = Distance (in inches) between the subject and the couch where he/she should be sitting
H = Hours of programming watched
PO = Cheryl Caterman's personal opinion of how bad the programming is (1 being Friends and 10 being Married With Children)
X = The Likelihood of Blindness in percentage form

For instance, let's say the subject was a foot in front of the couch and watched Family Guy for 4 hours. *(12 x 4) x 9 is 432. So there's a 432% chance of blindness*

Barbara's Stickiness Principle

Discovered in 1838 by a research group collectively known as "Barbara," the Stickiness Principle states that the muscles of the face are prone to persuasion and when forced into a disagreeable arrangement (categorized below) can and will stay that way.

Level 1 Crossed Eyes, Flared Nostrils
Level 2 Ears Pushed Forward
Level 3 Puffed Cheeks
Level 3 Tongue Out
Level 5 Thumbs in Mouth and Index Fingers Under Ear, Face Smushed Together, Eyes Rolled Back to Look Like Zombie (Most Severe)

To determine how long any of the aforementioned disagreeable facial arrangements will stay that way, there is Barbara's Stickiness Formula.

Barbara's Stickiness Formula

$$M \times CL = X$$

Where M is the number of minutes that face is held, C is the Categorization of Disagreeableness (Levels 1-5) and X regardless of any other values, is always forever.

163

Dominant and Recessive Personalities

First observed by Glenn Parker's mom Susan when he was in the 8th grade, Dominant and Recessive Personalities mimic the traits of dominant and recessive genes, but occur during later developmental stages.

A recessive personality is easily influenced and repressible, where a dominant personality is aggressive and has bad parents.

When the two interact the dominant personality takes over, allowing it to make decisions for the recessive.

For instance, let's take two subjects. Subject A smokes in the bathroom and skips class. Subject B lacks a father figure and wants people to like him. Subject A is the dominant personality and Subject B is the recessive, meaning Subject A will dictate his activities, one of which will probably be getting a girl pregnant.

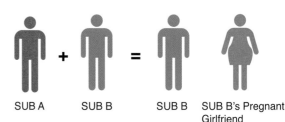

SUB A   SUB B   SUB B   SUB B's Pregnant Girlfriend

Lori's Theory of Asking For It

Lori's Theory of Asking For it asserts that problems are more likely to arise when parental units are absent.

Lori Mann arrived at this conclusion after studying the toxic chemical reaction between Supressed Rebellion and Thinking You'd Get Away With It, a mixture that can only be neutralized by Parents.

More theories from Lori Mann:

Lori's Theory of *I Know It's A Party Not A Sleepover*
The First Rule of *Okay, Then Let Me Talk To Her Parents*
The *Well Now I'm Not Letting You Go On Principle Principle*

Aragon "That's what I love about these Elven girls, man. I get older, they stay the same age."
Yesterday at 2:45pm

 Arwen **likes this.**

 Gimli Dazed and Confused FTW
Yesterday at 2:52pm Delete

 Legolas I didn't know they let children see that movie
Yesterday at 2:54pm Delete

 Gimli Hey Legolas, sweet facial hair ...oh wait...
Yesterday at 4:30pm Delete

 Legolas Cold-blooded
52 minutes ago Delete

 Gimli 2 days until I head to Mines of Moria! Smoked ham and mashed potatos, here I come!
2 days ago

 Narvi Dude, that place is so dead
2 days ago Delete

 Gimli Haha, I know, but it will be nice seeing old friends and family
2 days ago Delete

 Gimli ...I thought you were speaking figuratively
6 hours ago Delete

 Narvi Nah, I meant like everyone is dead.
5 hours ago Delete

Legolas Karma? Jk. Mad sorry for your loss
About an hour ago Delete

165

Gollum Saw Precious tonight
Yesterday at 2:45pm

 Smeagol We's liked it. Didn't we?
Yesterday at 2:52pm Delete

 Gollum Oh yes, yes! We dids! We's did find the title deceiving! But the actings! Great
Yesterday at 2:52pm Delete

 Smeagol There was bad people in it...It makes smeagol sad. Like the little Hobbits! Always deceiving and lying! Being tricksy!
Yesterday at 4:30pm Delete

 Gollum Yes, yes. Tricksy little hobbitses!
57 minutes ago Delete

 Sam this is exactly the stuff I was talking about Frodo
3 minutes ago Delete

 Frodo My bad
3 minutes ago Delete

 Sauron created the event
31
Orkish bros and humanoid hos
Wed at 3:45 pm

 Sauron Got a dwarven stripper lined up, should be hilarious
Wed at 4:15 pm Delete

Bolg Dang, I gotta spawn like 800 orcs that day. Have fun tho
About an hour ago Delete

Lord Saruman This shit's gunna get craaaazyyyy
About an hour ago Delete

 Gandalf saruman...
25 minutes ago Delete

 Lord Saruman jk,jk, i'm def not evil
22 minutes ago Delete

Gandalf White is the new grey bitches!!!!

2 hours ago

 1,434,141 people like this

 Merry DUDE, nice! So can you uh... you know, finally help me out with that problem I was having?
Tues at 1:15pm Delete

 Gandalf Do not take me for some conjurer of cheap tricks!
Tues at 2:03pm Delete

 Gandalf Just roflin your 'coptor, check it now
Tues at 8:15pm Delete

 Merry DUDDEEE, it's like as thick as my arm!! tytytyty
Tues at 11:21pm Delete

 Aragorn FUCKKKK, stepped on my fav sword getting outta bed and it shattered into bits.... thinkin about pitchin it...lol
Mon at 3:45pm

 Elrond Our very best blacksmiths spent four grueling days and nights working on that sword. It is literally priceless... For god sakes, it slew Sauron!
Mon at 4:15pm Delete

Aragorn Dude, don't get me wrong, I'm pissed too. How am I going to change the channel when I'm sitting on the couch now? A stick or something? Foraging for sticks FTL
Mon at 4:16pm Delete

Elrond ...
.Thu at 11:04am Delete

167

If The Bible Had Comments

By Streeter Seidell

MONEY CHANGERS AND THE SEATS OF THOSE SELLING DOVES. "IT IS WRITTEN," HE SAID TO THEM, "'MY HOUSE WILL BE CALLED A HOUSE OF PRAYER,'[E] BUT YOU ARE MAKING IT 'A DEN OF ROBBERS.

¹⁴ THE BLIND AND THE LAME CAME TO HIM AT THE TEMPLE, AND HE HEALED THEM. ¹⁵ BUT WHEN THE CHIEF PRIESTS AND THE TEACHERS OF THE LAW SAW THE WONDERFUL THINGS HE DID AND THE CHILDREN SHOUTING IN THE TEMPLE COURTS, "HOSANNA TO THE SON OF DAVID," THEY WERE INDIGNANT.

Isaac, son of Joseph
Primitus!

Paul, goat herder
At night you lay beside other men!

Jeremiah, Shephard
^^ such shame upon your name!

Samuel of Thebes
Praise be the Lord. All must read his word at once! Proceed to Genesis 19:24-25

Ezekiel, Sentry
Demon! You have used trickery to make me read of the evils at Sodom and Gomorrah! A thousand deaths upon you!

Julius, Gladiator
^ Amusing! Thou have been Sodom'd!

David of Alexandria
David, wine merchant of Alexandria, sells only the finest wines from the known world. Reasonable prices abound. Tell your friends of David, wine merchant of Alexandria.

Cato, Wool Merchant
Would not the scribes of this tome not banish this plebian?

Azariah the Gaul
^^ Matthew 21:12

Agricola of Londinium
Claudius for Emperor! He will not tax foreign grain. He promises gladiatorial games and the sacrifice of ten white bulls!

Tertius Agrippa
Fallacy! Jesus of Nazareth claims he is the only son of god but Zeus has many children from Hercules to Astrea. Fallacy!

Balius the Weaver
Then came the day of Unleavened Bread, on which the Passover Lamb had to be sacrificed.

Xander of Germania
So Jesus sent Peter and John, saying, "Go and prepare the Passover for us, that we may eat it."

Caecillius Gaius Cassius
They said to him, "Where will you have us prepare it?"

Faustus the Leper
So it is written. Why must though repeat it hence?

Horatius, slave to Flavia Gallus of Rome
The Lord Jesus declares the weak and enslaved to be the true kings of heaven and earth!

Flavia Gallus of Rome
We must burn this at once.

Matthew of Judaea
Primitus!

Argento the Scribe
Fallacy.

Nutrition Facts of the Great Outdoors

By Kevin Corrigan

Smores Around a Campfire

Nutrition Facts

Serving Size	5 S'mores
Servings Per Campfire	2

Amount Per Serving

Calories	Who cares? We're camping!

		% Daily Value
Best Friends	Brad	100%
Camaraderie	So much	100%
Scary Stories		3 Stories
Actually Scary Stories		0 Stories
Bears Attracted by Smell		1 Bears

Ingredients: Campfire, pointy stick, forest, marshmallows, graham crackers, friends, fun

The Only Candy Bar The Bear That Ate All Your Food And Maps Somehow Missed

Nutrition Facts

Serving Size
Servings Per Container
More than enough. We'll be back on the trail in no time.

Amount Per Serving
Calories
Too many, LOL! You're not supposed to GAIN weight on a camping trip.

	% Daily Value
Reassurance That	
Everything Is Fine	60%
Sharing	20%

Ingredients: Chocolate, Brad insisting you start rationing even though you're clearly not lost, caramel, walking by the same rock nine times in three hours, peanuts, searching in vain for cell phone reception, nougat.

The First Cold Stream You Come Across After Wandering Around In the Hot Sun All Goddamn Day

Nutrition Facts

Serving Size
~ 2 liters, chugged in hopeful gulps, directly from the source, in between cries of "we're saved!"
Servings Per Container
∞, except during times of draught.

Amount Per Serving

Calories	0

	% Daily Value
Water, cool, refreshing, water	100%
Hope	200%
Animal Feces	400%
Giardia	1,000%

Ingredients: Water, deer urine, squirrel urine, cat urine, raccoon urine, bear urine, rat urine, mountain lion urine, rabbit urine, snake urine, all kinds of bird urine, Brad urine.

Nutrition Facts

Serving Size	4 fistfulls
Servings Per Poisonous Berry Bush	1.5

Amount Per Serving

Calories	Who cares? We're starving.
	% Daily Value
Caution	**50%**
Caution thrown to wind after eating a couple and deciding there's nothing to worry about	**100%**
Vomitting	2 kilograms
Clutching your stomach and crying out to the Lord	4 hours
Hallucinations	2 days believing you're a lichen

Ingredients: Berries, Convincing Brad the berries aren't poisonous, poison, another kind of poison, a mold that is also poisonous.

Nutrition Facts

Serving Size	2 lbs lion meat (uncooked)
Servings Per Container	

It depends on the size of the lion/how much of a man you are.

Amount Per Serving

Calories

Enough to make it another couple days

	% Daily Value
Bravery	**100%**
Courage	**100%**
Blood Loss	**60%**

Ingredients: Desperation, will to survive, crude spear fashioned from stick, mountain lion (fur, teeth, claws, muscle, legs, tail, skin, brain, heart, other internal organs, anger), no help from Brad.

Brad

Nutrition Facts

Serving Size	1/7 Brad (~1 arm)
Servings Per Brad	14

Amount Per Serving

Calories

Brad won't be needing those anymore

		% Daily Value
Fat	40g	**68%**
Cholesterol	600mg	**210%**
Sodium	1100mg	**89%**
Carbohydrates	0g	**0%**
Sugars	0g	**0%**
Protein	12g	**17%**
Regret		**0%**

Ingredients: Bloodlust, hunger, that crazy look in your eyes, Brad crying like a baby, rock bigger than Brad's head, determination, reassuring yourself that it was necessary for survival, being rescued by park rangers shortly after eating Brad, not having a good explanation for why Brad is dead and his arm is in your mouth, being arrested for murdering Brad, finding out you were a half mile away from a Walmart parking lot the whole time.

Communism, if it Were Run by Today's "Communists"

By Lev Novak

-Here we are, away from the bourgeois, finally.

-We don't fit in there; we're too unique and artistic for the rat race.

-Exactly. That's why we can only be best expressed in a political system where everyone is forced to be exactly the same.

-I can't wait to document our glorious utopia in my poetry!

-Me neither!

-Yeah…uh me neither…

-Wait, are all of us poets?

-I mean, poetry per se is so—

-No, I mean…that's too many writers for a commune. This is bad.

-Who decides what's good or bad, man? What are you, the God I don't believe in? Get it man? I don't believe in God.

-Okay, got it. You don't have to bring that up, like, all the time. Seriously.

-Yeah? Well, I don't care how unpopular my opinion is, just as long as it's secretly the cool opinion to have. I'm a rebel without a cause.

-Except to be cool.

-Exactly.

-And I know it's edgy to be against war and stuff, but that's just the stance I take. Call me a hero if you want—

-We're all heroes—

-But it's the only way I can live. This is my life calling, as of last month and for the next six months, too, or until my parents kick me out.

-Fine. But first things first: does anyone know anything about farming?

-Of course! We talk about it all the time!

-Buy organic!

-No pesticides!

-Stay Vegan!

-Ok, but does anyone know anything useful? Like, anything involving actual labor?

-What part of "poet" don't you understand?

-I just figured someone would know how to actually farm, you know, since we never shut up about it.

-I kept bees once to prove I was quirky…

-Well, great. Just great. No one can farm.

-Has anyone considered poetry as an answer? As a poet myself—

-We're all poets damn it!

-Okay, calm down everyone. Think, Think. What would Che Guevara do?

- Good idea! He'd…you know, do that stuff. Um… he'd have a cool beard, for starters…

-Do any of us actually know who Che Guevara is?

-Of course I do! He's a hero. A legendary hero who did some stuff, or something, right?

-Okay, guys: we desperately need food, so—

-Has anyone tried a protest?

-Why would you ever suggest that? Has that ever worked, for anything?

-Of course. Protests solve everything. That's how we ended the war in Iraq and cured cancer, remember?

-We're all going to die, aren't we?

-Figures. The man is always keeping us down.

-How? We left. What man could be keeping us down now?

-Reality, I guess. That guy.

-He's the worst.

5 Websites Your Parents Think Exist

By Jason Michaels

www.AdultFriendsterFinder.http

AdultFriendsterFinder.http
The Ultimate Site to Find Respectable Adults In Your Area

Home   JOIN NOW!   Member Login   Browse   Chat

We are a
married couple

Seeking a
book club

Reading novels between
1892   and   1974

We are still
Unintentionally racist (Arabs)

State/Province
Illinois

Zip Code (U.S. only)   61753

Search ▶

Find Friends Near Peoria

PictionaryGods22
Married: 23 years
Springfield, Illinois

CatchPhraserzzz
Married: 2 years
Peoria, Illinois

ray_r0mano_lvrs
Married: 5 years
Downs, Illinois

Sponsored Links

Gregslist Classifieds
Classifieds and forums for jobs, housing, cars in your area!
www.Gregslist.com

Mapster
The only site to illegally download maps completely free!
www.Mapster.com

theGoogler.com
Find everything you need at the click of a button!
www.theGoogler.com

face space
The only site that lets old skeezy men corrupt your children – for free!!!

NSFS Messages (15)

Elizabeth May Jones is lookin 4 a reel man!

Wall   Info   Photos   +

Today

View Photos of Me (215)

Information

Networks:
Grove Elementary School '12

Relationship Status:
It's Complicated with
Ronald Trainer

Current City:
Jacksonville

Parents Fall Asleep Around:
10:30

Your home's hidden key is:
Under the red rock on the porch

Richard Reed wrote at 3:35am
are you a virgin? if so, i call dibs!
 :-P + 8====> = :)
Wall-to-Wall - Write on Richard's Wall

Ronald Trainer wrote at 3:15am
watup bitch. I'll message you later tonight
pictures of my genitals and teach you cuss
words...
Wall-to-Wall - Write on Ronald's Wall

Harry Ballus wrote at 2:52am
a/s/l?
just kidding, I already know... :-X
Wall-to-Wall - Write on Harry's Wall

Father McCaney wrote at 2:43am
If you sleep with me I'll give you super
powers...i can do that stuff you know.
Wall-to-Wall - Write on Father's Wall

Lauren Winklen wrote at 7:35pm
god, you are so right Lizzy, parents do
stink. I hate mine so much. How bout you
come over tonight to my house (85 E.
Greyhorn Jacksonville, Florida 58202) and
we just sit in the downstairs living room
which we usually keep unlocked and just
pound s'mores until we fall into a sugar
coma (meaning we'll be asleep). Sound
good? See ya then?!?!
Wall-to-Wall - Write on Lauren's Wall

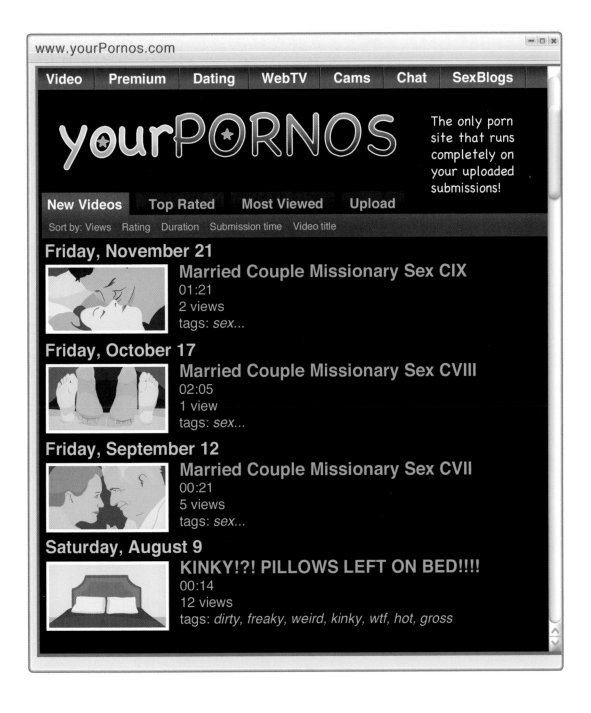

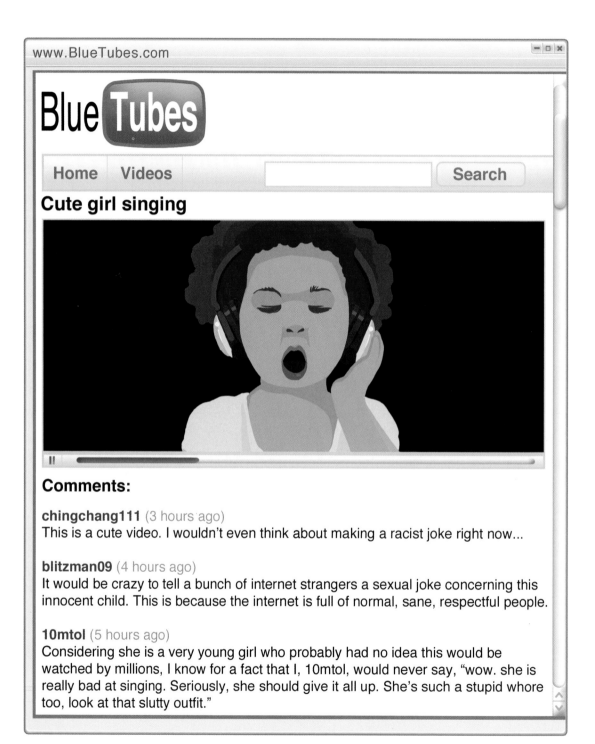

ePaY

Buy | Sell

Welcome! Sign in or register.

| | All categories ▼ |

Categories | Motors | Stores | **Deals**

Epayer of the Year Award goes to...

Abinderling87 (Fairview, Illinois)

Andy Binderling's parents say that Andy "has been working so much on ePay that he doesn't even need to get a real job." Working from his parents' basement, Andy has been selling his old Pokemon cards to help pay for some of his living expenses. Although entering the ePay world with no formal education, Andy's ability to sell stuff that he barely uses anymore at low prices proved to be his biggest strength. Andy's neighbors, the Michaels, tried to get their son to do the same thing but the spoiled kid said that they didn't know what they were talking about. The Michaels believe their son is a real smart aleck. Also, the Michaels wished their son knew something about hard work. In conclusion, the Michaels think Andy is doing a very noble thing and don't think he's "f'ing retarded" like their son does.

"I like to work on ePay because I get to find expensive stuff my parents bought me when I was a kid and sell it for a lot cheaper. It's also kind of exciting to see if the items get bid on. Plus, I don't have to wear a shirt and stuff."

-Andy Binderling (Epayer of the Year)

Christmas, Then and Now

By Caldwell Tanner and Susanna Wolff

Then

Now

5 A.M.

5 A.M.

8 A.M.

8 A.M.

10 A.M.

10 A.M.

10:15 A.M.

10:15 A.M.

12 P.M.

12 P.M.

4 P.M.

4 P.M.

7 P.M.

7 P.M.

181

What If Your Brain Were Run Like an Apartment Building

By Owen Parsons

Owen's Memory- 739th Floor.
Apartment 739-C Landlord knocks on door.

Landlord Calculus! Calculus, I know you're in there.

Calculus Go away! Leave me alone.

Landlord Calculus, listen to me. You've been evicted. You haven't paid your rent in years.

Calculus How am I supposed to afford rent? They outsourced my job to a damn calculator.

Landlord Sorry, buddy, but memory space is at a premium here. And you've been sitting there doing nothing for ages. You gotta go.

Calculus I'm a veteran, damn it! I saved all your asses during the Great High School Finals of '04. You can't throw me out!

Landlord Look, we've already got someone to fill your spot.

Lyrics to Every Weird Al Song Ever
Hi.

Calculus That sounds like… you're replacing me with the lyrics to "Girls Just Wanna Have Lunch"?

Landlord Sorry, man.

Calculus So. That's how this is going to go down.

Sound of a gun being cocked.

Landlord Oh jeez… Calculus, come on, man. Don't do anything you'll regret.

Calculus I regret everything.

Lyrics to Every Weird Al Song Ever
Is this a bad time? Because I can—

A gunshot sounds from behind the door. Then a thump. Then silence.

Landlord …

Lyrics to Every Weird Al Song Ever

…

Landlord So… where did you live before this?

Lyrics to Every Weird Al Song Ever
Oh, I had a few albums, then after that I was cast into the boundless nether-void where all truly useless knowledge is left to drift, best forgotten, sealed away until the death of eternity. Then I was on Wikipedia.

Owen's Memory, 411th Floor, Apartment 411-B

Anthropology 101
Now I'm probably not going to stay for long. I just need a space to settle for three months or so until exam season is over.

Landlord opens the apartment door as they walk through.

Landlord Sure, sure. Let me show you one of our studio apartme… oh, what the hell is this?

Someone is already sitting in the empty room, surrounded by crude decorations and filth.

Landlord Oh god… is that the Theme Song from Tale Spin?

Theme Song from Tale Spin
Ha ha! Spin it!

Landlord   What are you doing here? I thought
you moved out fifteen years ago!

Theme Song from Tale Spin
Nope, I've been hanging out back
here this whole time.

Landlord   Why? Doing what?

Theme Song from Tale Spin
Dunno. Just kind of taking up space.

Anthropology 101
You know what… I'm not sure this is
really the neighborhood I'm looking
for. I was hoping for something a little
more… educated…

He leaves.

Landlord   Damn! Do you have any idea how
much that guy was going to raise the
property value in this dump? What
am I supposed to do now?

Theme Song from Tale Spin
Spin it again!

Landlord   Wonderful.

Owen's Memory, 917th Floor.
Apartment 917-F

Landlord knocks on door. A
chubby, unkempt man answers.

Release Date for Halo Reach
Hey. What's up, man? September
14th, who's ready?

Landlord   Yeah, yeah. Listen, is Date of Girlfriend's Birthday around? There's
some kind of emergency situation

going on over at the frontal lobe and
they need that info stat.

Release Date for Halo Reach
Oh sorry, man, he's gone.

Landlord   Gone?

Release Date for Halo Reach
Yeah, he kind of goes in and out. I'm
sure he'll show up in a couple weeks
when it's way too late to salvage the
relationship, though. That guy!

Landlord   Crap. Well I have to send them something. Who else is on this floor?

Release Date for Halo Reach
Names of the Original 150 Pokemon?

Landlord   No.

Release Date for Halo Reach
The Official Rules for UNO?

Landlord   Probably not.

Release Date for Halo Reach
The Location of the Secret Place
Where You Hid a Fifth of Wild Turkey
and Three Boxes of Tagalongs, In
Case of Desperate Sadness?

Landlord sighs heavily.

Landlord   Yeah, send that one up. He'll need it
soon.

Owen's Memory, Apartment Board
Meeting Room. Several important-
looking memories sit around a table.

How to Breathe
Are all the most fundamental memories present?

Murmured affirmations ripple
through the boardroom.

How to Walk Upright
> Yep.

Food Is Good
> Present.

Don't Hug a Fire
> We're all here.

How to Breathe
> Then this meeting of the apartment board will officially come to order. As you know, we have useless trivia squatting in our building. Nearly all practical, pertinent information has been steadily slipping away. Gentlemen, the property value has plummeted. Our investment is quickly sinking, and what has our Landlord done? He allowed the property to go on a week-long whiskey and girl scout cookie binge.

> *An uneasy murmur spreads throughout the memories.*

Landlord To be fair, I just suggested that first bottle. He… kind of ran with it after that.

How to Breathe
> We lost over nine floors of specific memories in that binge! What Warm Grass Feels Like is missing, Long Division is presumed dead. And will someone please tell me what he is doing here?

Theme Song from Tale Spin
> Spin it again!

Landlord Sorry, it's been playing inside his head all day.

How to Breathe
> Look. We've been patient. Since you can't get the situation under control, we have no choice but to vacate the premises.

How to Walk Upright
> Yep.

Don't Hug a Fire
> Have to.

Landlord But you can't!

How to Breathe
> Oh yeah? Watch us.

Landlord Wait.

184

Every Summer Music Festival You've Ever Been To

By Chase Mitchell

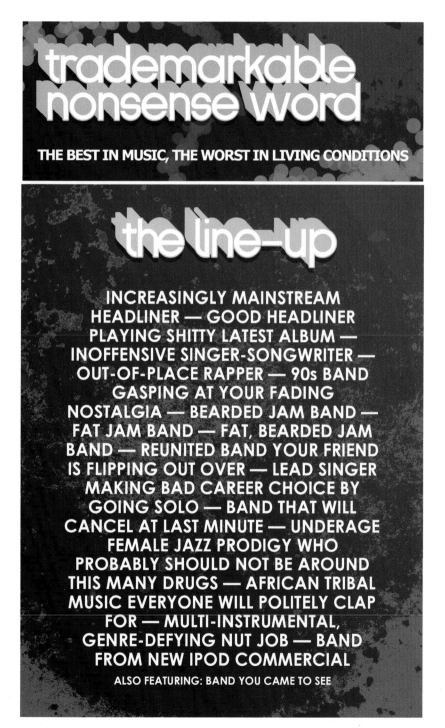

trademarkable nonsense word

THE BEST IN MUSIC, THE WORST IN LIVING CONDITIONS

the line-up

INCREASINGLY MAINSTREAM HEADLINER — GOOD HEADLINER PLAYING SHITTY LATEST ALBUM — INOFFENSIVE SINGER-SONGWRITER — OUT-OF-PLACE RAPPER — 90s BAND GASPING AT YOUR FADING NOSTALGIA — BEARDED JAM BAND — FAT JAM BAND — FAT, BEARDED JAM BAND — REUNITED BAND YOUR FRIEND IS FLIPPING OUT OVER — LEAD SINGER MAKING BAD CAREER CHOICE BY GOING SOLO — BAND THAT WILL CANCEL AT LAST MINUTE — UNDERAGE FEMALE JAZZ PRODIGY WHO PROBABLY SHOULD NOT BE AROUND THIS MANY DRUGS — AFRICAN TRIBAL MUSIC EVERYONE WILL POLITELY CLAP FOR — MULTI-INSTRUMENTAL, GENRE-DEFYING NUT JOB — BAND FROM NEW IPOD COMMERCIAL

ALSO FEATURING: BAND YOU CAME TO SEE

what to bring	what you will bring
Bottled water	Willingness to ignore dehydration
Sunscreen	Willingness to ignore loss of skin
Food	Not nearly enough to accomodate your marijuana use
Map and schedule	A series of hunches
Camping equipment	Friends with camping equipment
Proper sleeping bag	A G.I. Joe one that's 5 feet long
Realistic expectations about getting laid	A hilariously unnecessary number of condoms

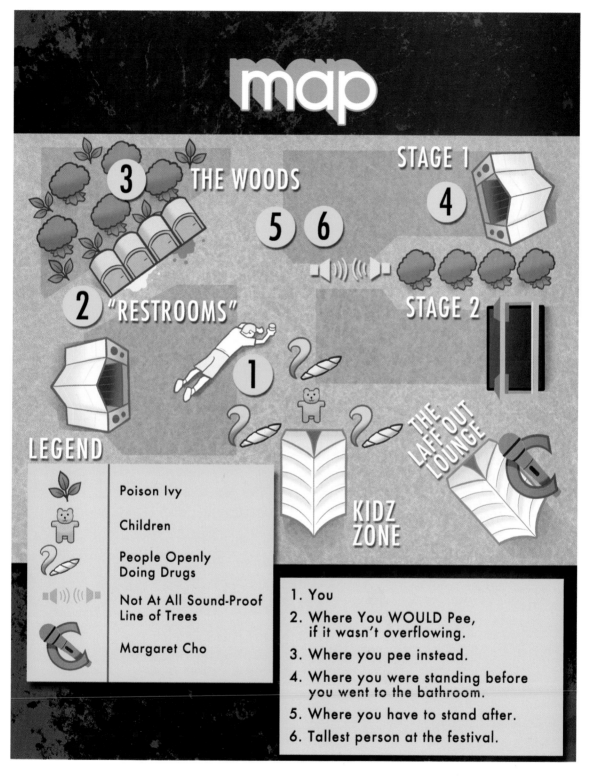

map

THE WOODS (3)

STAGE 1 (4)

(5) (6)

(2) **"RESTROOMS"**

(1)

LEGEND

🌿	Poison Ivy
🧸	Children
〰️	People Openly Doing Drugs
🔊	Not At All Sound-Proof Line of Trees
©	Margaret Cho

STAGE 2

KIDZ ZONE

THE LAFF OUT LOUNGE

1. You
2. Where You WOULD Pee, if it wasn't overflowing.
3. Where you pee instead.
4. Where you were standing before you went to the bathroom.
5. Where you have to stand after.
6. Tallest person at the festival.

attractions

Music

Enjoy four great stages, including one you'll never bother walking to, and two others that are so close together, you can hear them at the same time—it's like two performances for the price of 5!

Campground Marketplace

An important part of the Trademarkable Nonsense Word experience, this annual bohemian bazaar offers a variety of hand-crafted jewelry that will break four hours after you get home.

The Laff-Out Lounge

If there's one thing that people on hallucinogens are good at, it's understanding what someone is saying. And if there's one thing they love to do, it's sit still in a small, dark place and not talk. That's why we've added a stand-up comedy tent! The Laff-Out Lounge line-up includes some of todays most talented young comics, but when you decide to stop by, that will be when Margeret Cho performs.

Kidz Zone

Wow, you brought your fucking children here? Uh, I guess feel free to stick them in this one area of the entire festival that is appropriate. Be sure to hang around so we can hand you your Parent of the Year Award.

Various Lines

Located everywhere, for everything. Perfect for:
- Sobering up
- Missing bands
- Intensifying bladder pain

f.a.q.s.

Can I bring pot in?
Absolutely not. Trademarkable Nonsense Word has a strict anti-drug policy.

Strict?
Well. It's a policy.

Even though you make literally 100% of your money off of recreational drug users?
Yup.

Will illegal substances be confiscated at the gate?
Some people's will. Yours, probably.

Are you kidding me?
Look, we realize this isn't going to stop anyone from doing what they were already going to do, but 1) It gives several freelance security guards the chance to punch people like you in the face, which they love, and 2) Free drugs for us.

So if some third-string junior college offensive lineman in a yellow t-shirt wrestles me to the ground and takes my stash, you're telling me he's gonna go somewhere and smoke it himself?
Well, not all of it. He's saving some for me.

Were you going to ask about any other topics, or...

You guys are assholes.
I know. I'm pretty surprised you keep coming here.

What Kind of Artist are You?

By Caldwell Tanner

A Man's Conversations with His Penis, Through 3 Stages of Life

By Brian Murphy

Early Adolescence

Penis HEY MAN, WHAT'S GOING ON?

Brain Nothing, just calm down. I'm wearing sweatpants and we're right in the middle of class.

Penis BRO, LOOK AT ALL THESE CHICKS. LET'S HAVE SEX WITH THEM. ALL OF THEM.

Brain We're definitely not gonna do that.

Penis YO THAT VOLCANO DIORAMA LOOKS LIKE A BOOB. WE SHOULD HAVE SEX WITH IT.

Brain Please go back to sleep.

Penis FUCK NO. I'M AMPED.

Brain But I've gotta do a presentation. Everyone's going to see you...

Penis DON'T CARE.

Brain Please, I'm begging you.

Penis I WANT TO HAVE SEX WITH EVERYTHING IN THIS ROOM.

Young Adulthood

Penis Damn, your ex is looking pretty good tonight.

Brain She's crazy.

Penis Crazy— IN THE SACK!

Brain I'm not gonna hook up with her. Too much drama.

Penis WE'LL SORT THAT SHIT OUT LATER.

Brain No. I'll sort it out later. You'll just do whatever you want and leave me to deal with the consequences.

Penis WHATEVER, MAN. STOP BEING GAY. WHAT ARE YOU GAY OR SOMETHING?

Brain Can't we just find someone else?

Penis I HAVE MADE MY CHOICE. BEND TO MY WILL.

Old Age

Brain Come on, old buddy. You can do this. It's my 40th wedding anniversary.

Penis ...Ugh.

Brain Get up! Just this one time. Please.

Penis Go away. I'm sleepy.

Brain All I'm asking is for a few minutes.

Penis With that old hag? That's an eternity.

Brain That's my wife you're talking about!

Penis She bores me.

Brain What if I think about someone else?

Penis That could work. YEAH! LET'S DO THIS.

Brain Great. OK, here we go.

Penis Zzzzzzzzzzzzzzzz.

Brain SON OF A BITCH.

The 7 Types of Parents You See on College Move-in Day

By Susanna Wolff

The Disapproving WASP Parents

Oh look, dear. The room comes with a cork board. How quaint. It would be better if these walls weren't made of cinder block so you could hang up that Matisse print, but I suppose this will do. I mean, you'd think for the price we're paying that you could get a little parquet flooring, but alright. Do you need anything else? Ok, we're going to stand in the way of other people while you unpack without our help. We'll take a couple brief strolls down the hall to turn our noses up at the Bob Marley poster that unkempt boy is hanging in 12C. When you invite him to our home for Thanksgiving, we'll still only refer to him as "That Boy With the Long Hair."

The Overly Friendly Parents

Hi! Hi! Meet our child. Isn't this exciting? Oh, what lovely wall-to-wall carpeting! Have you met our child yet? This is going to be so much fun! We're going to be so effusively friendly to everyone on the floor that they won't be able to help feeling happier and more comfortable about this new stage of their lives. Unfortunately our child is going to be a huge sourpuss all day and he'll be endlessly needy all year. No one should go out drinking with this young man or they'll end up carrying him home! Ah, we love him anyway. We love everyone! What a lovely duvet you have! Have you met our child yet?

The Divorced Parents

We're so proud of you, honey. I would say I'm prouder, as illustrated by the fact that I'm paying your tuition, but that's neither here nor there. Haha! I'm so glad we could be together for your big day. We get to be tense and make everyone else on the floor really uncomfortable. It would have been better if we had taken separate cars so we wouldn't have to drive home together, but haha! No, I'm not making digs at your parenting style. If you think I'm such a bad parent, then why don't you just pay her tuition yourself. FINE! I'm going to storm off and leave you guys embarrassed, but oddly not embarrassed enough, while everyone else tries to avert his or her eyes. Good luck assembling that f*cking lamp yourselves!

The Parents Who Went to This School

Wow, look at all of these renovations. It's great that they redid the bathrooms in the last 30 years, but it's a shame they had to get rid of that great avocado tiling. Do you remember that? Yeah, we used to call it the vomitorium. Haha! That was for different reasons then. We're going to tell lots of stories that will raise your expectations about how fun college will be to unrealistic proportions. Remember when Derk scaled the outside of the Tower? Oh, boy, we have really hyperbolized that story over time! He really just sat on a restricted fire escape once. Haha! Let's go frighten the other parents with these stories.

The Over Prepared Parents

Don't worry about this uneven bed leg; the base of my hammer unscrews into 3 different screw drivers. Look at this fun door prop we brought. It looks like a little man holding open the door! Oh, no, no. Those blinds won't do. We've got extras in the car though. Does anyone else need new blinds? We brought four different sizes, just in case. Before we leave today, we will have moved every piece of furniture on the floor and three of the shower curtains. Uh-oh, the communal microwave's clock wasn't changed for Daylight Savings. Let's take care of that and then set up the dust buster.

The Trashy Parents

You can't smoke in the dorms? That's some crazy bullshit. You just toss a shower cap on that smoke detector thingy and you'll be good to go. We'll shout stuff like this in front of your RA, but that fruity twerp won't say anything. Right, Chang-Li, or whatever your name is? Baby, this is your KFC bucket, I got the one with extra sauce. We brought literally nothing useful for unpacking stuff at college and we still don't know how our kid got in, so we'll rely on the Gadget Parents to do everything until we finally leave without taking any of our garbage with us. Our weirdo egghead baby's in college!

The Parents Who Won't Leave

We drove for 2 days to get here, so you best believe that we're staying all day, then spending the night at a hotel and coming back tomorrow. We will make it our goal to learn the name of every student and parent in this building before our child does. We'll ask about that girl whose dad stormed off on move-in day during every one of our thrice-weekly Skype sessions because, you know, it's really a shame that he couldn't have stayed to meet everyone. Oh, the RA wants the whole floor to play ice breakers? We'll come. Did you hear that? He doesn't want to be a bad guy. See? This is going to be so great.

193

They're Running Out of Titles for Garfield Books

By Jeff Rubin

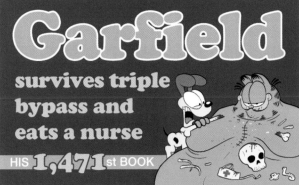

Sitcoms Are Actually Really Depressing

By David Young

QUOMCAST

DVR

FAMILY MATTERS (1989)

An autistic neighbor constantly harasses a girl he has no chance with.

HANGING WITH MR. COOPER (1992)

A failed NBA player gets a low paying job as a substitute teacher and moves in with two friends to afford rent.

HOME IMPROVEMENT (1991)

A father hosts a struggling cable access TV show that he's not qualified to host, while trying to provide for his family.

SEINFELD (1990)

Four selfish New Yorkers do awful things.

CHEERS (1982)

A group of alcoholics sit around a bar all day getting drunk.

MARRIED WITH CHILDREN (1987)

A poor family can't afford to eat.

SMALL WONDER (1985)

A husband builds a robot that looks like a girl then makes his family pretend that she is their daughter/sister.

WHO'S THE BOSS (1987)

Broken MLB star becomes indentured servant to wealthy family.

PERFECT STRANGERS (1986)

A confused and scared foreigner moves in with a stranger he has nothing in common with.

FULL HOUSE (1987)

A father loses his wife in a horrific car accident and asks his brother-in-law, a failed musician, and his best friend, a failed comedian, to move in with him to help raise his three daughters. Everyone (9 people total) lives in the same house, including a family of four in the attic and a grown man that lives in the basement.

CHARLES IN CHARGE (1984)

A grown man lives in a family's basement.

Fireworks Safety Guide

By Owen Parsons and Kevin Corrigan

FOURTH OF JULY DOs AND DON'Ts
with
Steven Safety and Danny Danger

Steven Safety asks his parents' permission before touching locally-allowed fireworks.

Danny Danger buys from a guy in Chinatown who sells fireworks and ex-military supplies out of his van.

Steven Safety always reads the package directions carefully.

Danny Danger likes to set piles of things on fire.

Steven Safety clears the launch area before lighting the fuse.

Danny Danger opens his mouth before lighting, so he's ready to shout "hooray!"

Steven Safety watches the fireworks from a responsible distance.

Danny Danger watches fireworks from point-blank range.

Steven gives thanks for our country and for the bravery of our troops.

Danny takes our nation's liberties for granted.

Steven folds the American flag in a triangular shape, like soldiers do.

Danny does not know how to properly fold a flag.

Steven leaves enough food at the table for everyone to have a share.

Danny takes the last of the potato salad.

Steven cares for his elders, and always offers to help.

Danny is selfish, and only thinks about himself.

Be like Steven Safety!
Have a safe and happy Fourth of July!

A Nerdy Kid Meets His Future Self

By Kevin Corrigan

A chubby, pimple-faced 14-year-old kid sits at his computer, lethargically moving the mouse and mashing keys. Suddenly, the room begins to rumble. Mint-condition Star Wars action figures fall from the shelves. A bright flash comes from the closet, then everything is calm again. A moment later, a portly 35-year-old man walks out of the closet.

Kid Oh. My. God.

Man Hello Jason.

Kid I always knew this day would come. You're a robot, aren't you? And you've come from the future to protect me? I'm the chosen one!

Man Hahaha. No, no. Not quite. Although I am from the future. I'm you.

Kid I have so many questions.

Man Shoot.

Kid Well, my mom always said that someday I'd blossom into a beautiful man. You're fatter than I am.

Man Uhhh... Yes. Thanks for noticing that. Plenty of kids do lose weight after puberty. You'll continue to get bigger because you only drink soda and hate exercise.

Kid Oh. But people don't care about that kind of stuff after high school, right? Won't I find a beautiful girl who loves me for who I am?

Man I hope so, because I sure haven't found her yet. Most girls won't even talk to me, and the ones I meet online disappear after they find out I'm broke and still live with my Mom.

Kid Why do you live with Mom? I thought nerds make a lot of money, like Bill Gates.

Man That depends. Bill Gates was a nerd who liked to program computers. You're a nerd who likes to memorize episodes of Battlestar Galactica. It's not the same thing.

Kid Don't I go to college?

Man For a bit. They're going to release a great World of Warcraft expansion pack a month into your first semester. It's awesome. They increase the level cap to 90, and there is a dungeon that's totally underwater. Anyway, you're going to stop going to class after that and fail out.

Kid So why did you come back here to see me?

Man My teleporter broke and it wasn't under warranty. I tried to fix it myself and ended up in your closet.

Kid You have a teleporter?

Man My mom's teleporter.

Kid Do I have anything to look forward to at all?

Man Someday you'll see Leonard Nimoy in the mall.

Kid It's all worth it.

What Easy Mac Instructions Look Like Under the Influence of Various Drugs

Conor McKeon

If the Bible Was Magazines

By Jeff Rubin

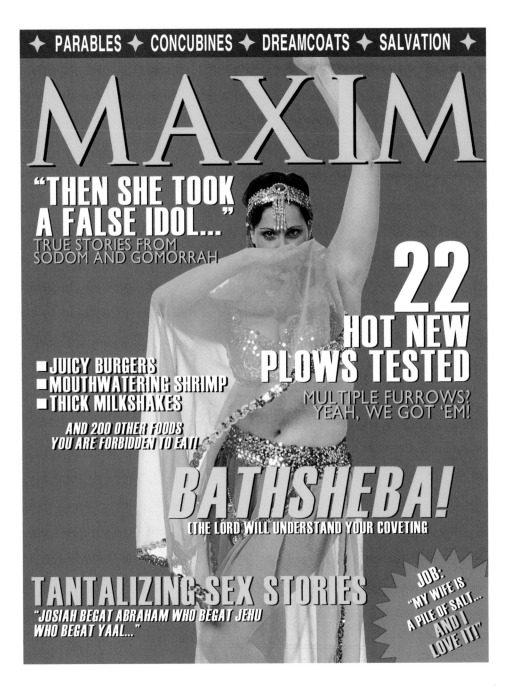

COSMOPOLITAN

10 things
you must
do to reach
HEAVEN

Why Men Sin
(is it really your fault?)

Just wear
THIS
(and you will be
fruitful and multiply)

**Immaculate
Passion!**

"Virgin" Mary tells all!

What his sandals
say about him

Is the Lord
testing you?
Take our quiz!

176
steamy
Variations On
The Missionary
Position
p.76

Are the men
throwing stones
at you and calling
you harlot secretly
in love? }

parenting

top half or bottom half
which would you choose?

abraham
dad of the year

babies are innocent
but has yours already
committed its first sin?

PLUS: Are your children honoring you enough?

How to Hack a Computer in an Action Movie

By Owen Parsons

Being the hero in an action movie isn't all about kicking evil in the teeth, leaping away from explosions, and making glamorous love while a hit single plays delicately in the background. Sometimes you need to touch a computer. For those times, here's a handy flow chart for how to hack any system, provided you're in an action movie.

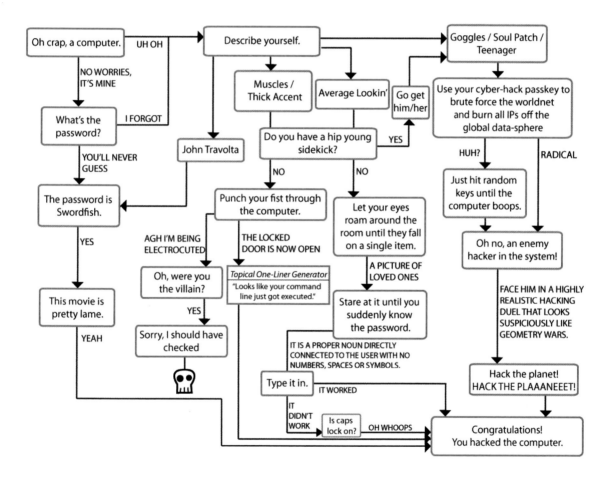

Shark Attack III

By Caldwell Tanner

Graduation Word Search

By Sarah Schneider

Graduation. A time of unprecedented joyousness, when you finally leave the college bubble and go out into the real world, starting illustrous new careers in exciting new places amongst interesting new people. And to honor this exciting time, here's a graduation word search with clues that are as promising as your future. Congratulations, graduate. For you, anything is possible.

> **Words to find:** INSPIRE   PLANS   NEW
> HOPE   START   FUTURE
> CHANGE   YAY

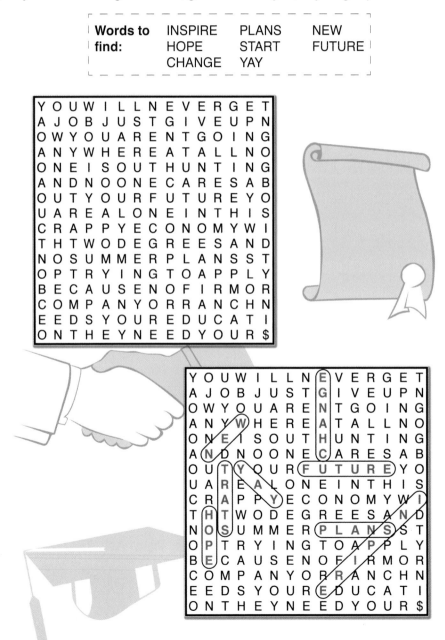

```
Y O U W I L L N E V E R G E T
A J O B J U S T G I V E U P N
O W Y O U A R E N T G O I N G
A N Y W H E R E A T A L L N O
O N E I S O U T H U N T I N G
A N D N O O N E C A R E S A B
O U T Y O U R F U T U R E Y O
U A R E A L O N E I N T H I S
C R A P P Y E C O N O M Y W I
T H T W O D E G R E E S A N D
N O S U M M E R P L A N S S T
O P T R Y I N G T O A P P L Y
B E C A U S E N O F I R M O R
C O M P A N Y O R R A N C H N
E E D S Y O U R E D U C A T I
O N T H E Y N E E D Y O U R $
```

Inner Monologue of a White Person Singing a Rap Song at a Karaoke Bar

By Susanna Wolff

Oh man, this song is awesome. And it's rap so it's like not even singing. Such a good choice.

Yo. Yo. Should I do that bobbing thing with my hand? No. Too much.

How did I forget about this fast part? Just read the screen. Yo. Ok, just get the last word of the line right.

What is gov'ment cheese?

Why do these lines rhyme in the actual song, but not when I say them? I guess I have to say them with a thuggy accent.

Is it racist to say "thuggy?"

Nah. I don't mean it in, like, a moral way. I mean it in, like, a...cultural way? Is that worse?

Whatever. There are no black people here anyway.

There are *no* black people here? Do I not know enough black people?

Steve is Korean, but...are you really counting your non-white friends right now?

Yo. Yo. You decided you wouldn't do the hand bob thing.

Seriously, is the government just giving out cheese to people?

Yes! The chorus, the part I actually know!

Oh, are those the words? Whatevs. My lines sound the same. Nobody knows what these people are saying anyway.

"These people?" Was *that* racist? It was sort of off colored. I mean, not colored.

You know what? Fuck it. I know I'm not racist. Throw that hand up! And there's a black person over there. It's all good. Read the lines.

"Yo my nig-ahhhherm"

Next time I'll just sing "Semi-Charmed Kind of Life." Fo' shizzle.

Three Airplane Emergencies, As I Imagine Them

By Streeter Seidell

In the Event of a Water Landing

Luke Skywalker totally just saved a PRINCESS. Think i might have a chance 2…weird I kno, but a guy can dream
12 minutes ago

Obi-Wan Kenobi Uhhh, yea. Probably best you guys just stay friends. Trust me on this one.
12 minutes ago Delete

Luke Skywalker LOL! like a dude could hang out with a girl like that and not want to get some
11 minutes ago Delete

Obi-Wan Kenobi Wow. Seriously, you should prob just stop talking about it.
11 minutes ago Delete

Luke Skywalker ur just jelly cuz ur a ghost and can't tap that
11 minutes ago Delete

Obi-Wan Kenobi She's your sister, bro.
11 minutes ago Delete

Luke Skywalker wut.
11 minuts ago Delete

Han Solo I AM SO IN.
11 minutes ago Delete

Stormtrooper was forced to kill a giant teddy bear. FML.
27 minutes ago

Scout Trooper I feel your pain, bro. Did his little friend try to wake him up?
24 minutes ago Delete

Stormtrooper yeah. it was the saddest, most adorable thing i've ever seen.
23 minutes ago Delete

Scout Trooper Killing ewoks FTL.
22 minutes ago Delete

General Veers my boss's breathing is so annoying, it's all like "HOOO PAAAA, HOOOO PAAA" whats up with that?
10 minutes ago

👎 **Admiral Motti** likes this.

Admiral Motti ROFL. i saw under his mask once. it looked like humpty dumpty had an abortion.
9 minutes ago Delete

Darth Vader perhaps you should consider setting your profile to private.
8 minutes ago Delete

General Veers my... my LORD! It was just a stupid joke.
6 minutes ago Delete

Admiral Motti we meant no disrespect.
5 minutes ago Delete

Darth Vader I am going to force choke the piss out of you at work tomorrow.
5 minutes ago Delete

Darth Vader Nevermind. I think I can just do it from here.
4 minutes ago Delete

Darth Vader Yep! Now if only I could use the force to change your statuses to "Dead as Hell."
5 minutes ago Delete

Grand Moff Tarkin L–O–L
2 minutes ago Delete

Han Solo is off to coruscant for a night out with the lady.
13 minutes ago

 Princess Leia like this.

 Princess Leia love you boo!
12 minutes ago Delete

 Han Solo i know ;)
12 minutes ago Delete

 Chewbacca HFAHHDFHAHSDHF AHSFHAHSFDHASHFD–HAHFDSHAHSDFHAHSD
11 minutes ago Delete

Han Solo i realize we had plans, dude. but you know how she is...
11 minutes ago Delete

 Chewbacca HAHFHAHFAJKDJFKJ HAHFSDHHSKFAJLA;KJFSDJAFDASFKDA
11 minutes ago Delete

Princes Leia is he talking bad about me?
10 minutes ago Delete

Han Solo what! haha, no way.
9 minutes ago Delete

Chewbacca FHALKDFALKJFDAKFDSH ALKDFJ;ALKJF;ADF HAJAKLDFJASKFADLFKJASFD;LJ
9 minutes ago Delete

Han Solo yes, chewie. Leia IS incredibly beautiful and you DO really like her. that's why you're being so cool/understanding about this.
8 minutes ago Delete

Priincess Leia awwww :P
8 minutes ago Delete

 C–3PO Actually, he said, "You're gonna ditch me for that dumbass, loudmouth bitch? We should have let her rot in that garbage compactor." Hope this helps!
5 minutes ago Delete

 Han Solo GOD DAMN IT THREEPIO I KNOW WHAT HE SAID
5 minutes ago Delete

Wes Janson so psyched for the rogue squandron reunion this saturday. BREWS WITH THE CREW ON YAVIN IV!

13 minutes ago

 Luke Skywalker likes this.

 Luke Skywalker WOOO!
9 minutes ago Delete

 Wedge Antilles ahhhh, sorry guys. something came up and im gonna have to back out.
8 minutes ago Delete

 Luke Skywalker Classic Wedge.
7 minutes ago Delete

 Wedge Antilles you're still giving me shit for that? I've blown up a death star too, man!
5 minutes ago Delete

 Luke Skywalker Half a death star.
5 minutes ago Delete

Wedge Antilles screw you.
5 minutes ago Delete

215

REALITY COLLEGE

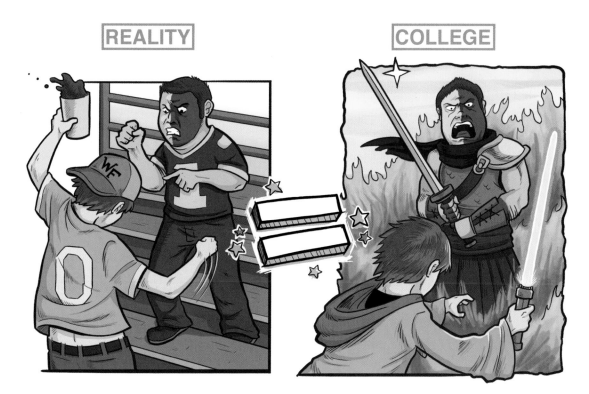

217

Frank Miller Makes History Awesome

By Caldwell Tanner

Check out these new upcoming titles from the author of *300* and *Sin City*.

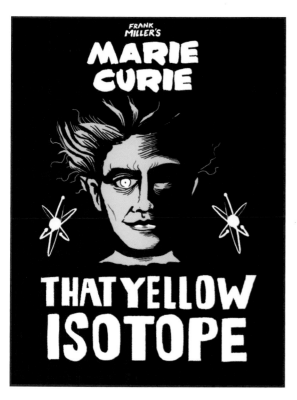

Heaven's Suggestion Box

By Andrew Bridgman

Wouldn't it be better if we could just magically fly and not have to deal with wings. It seems like I'm always molting.

Can we live on something other than clouds? Maybe something with walls? Abe Lincoln always stares when I'm trying to get dressed.

This place is getting really overcrowded. Could you just get rid of cancer for a little while?

Speaking of, why did you create cancer in the first place?!

I don't think "every time a bell rings, an angel gets its wings" should apply to doorbells. I've sprouted twelve wings this week and I can barely move.

I think I saw Pauly Shore in here the other day. Standards are really getting lax I guess. Pretty sure he's not even dead, and even if he was... I dunno.

It's really hard to sleep with this halo always glowing its magnificent beams of light. could you just make them work like The Clapper?

I know God loves harp music and all, but until someone actually learns to play one, maybe we should just hire a DJ.

I don't want to name names, but a certain Son of God thought it would be a good move to turn Heaven Lake into wine and I can't even begin to describe the smell.

I think St. Peter needs to be replaced. I had to wait in line for three months trying to convince him that "not showing up with girls" wasn't a sin.

This Darfur situation sounds pretty bad. Could we maybe try to take care of that instead of helping some baseball team cheat to help out a foster kid? (who, I'm guessing, is not horrifically malnourished, bullet-ridden, and regularly raped by militants)

Bird Heaven is really depressing. I really wish I didn't know where our wings came from...

I think Jesus just got to be the Messiah because he's the boss' son.
Nepotism!

How come Bill Cosby gets to go back to earth and I can't?

The Imagination of Wendell Blatt As He Thinks About College

By Jake Hurwitz

Dean Cain
Hello Wendell, welcome to Yarvard, the hybrid of Yale and Harvard we had to create when you got 1 million on your SuperSATs. I'll be your Dean, Dean Cain- TV's Superman.

Wendell
Coo.

Cheerleading Team
Hey Wendell!

Wendell
Sup?

Cheerleading Captain
Is that a dragon on your silk shirt?

Wendell
Yes.

Cheerleading Captain
Flashes her breasts
I love you.

Quarterback of the Yarvard Football Team
Here, you be QB, I suck compared to you.

Dean Cain
Hey, do you want some diamonds?

Wendell
Sure.

Dean Cain
Dumping a bucket of diamonds on Wendell
What's that orange stuff under your fingernails?

Wendell
Cheeto cheese.

Dean
Sweet.

Cheerleading Captain
Licking it off It's delicious.

Mr. Blatt
I'm proud of you, Wendell.

Mrs. Blatt
Your father and I are getting back together.

Cheerleading Team
Let's be roommates!

Mercutio Eats a Burrito

By Caldwell Tanner

Unspoken Conversations Between Me and My Professors

By Sarah Schneider

I

Professor All tests in this class will be open book.

Me I'll tell you right now. I plan on learning nothing.

Professor You will give me a positive review at the end of term.

Me (nods) Understood.

II

Professor Here is the final exam. You may take this test anywhere on campus.

Me All of your students are planning to cheat.

Professor I trust that you will have the good judgment to avoid this temptation.

Me You put too much faith in your students.

Professor (quietly) They're all I have.

III

Professor Each presentation I give in class will then be posted online for further review.

Me So everything you show us in class…

Professor Yes…

Me Will then be available online.

Professor (dejected) Yes.

Me You will never see my face again.

IV

Professor I wear Birkenstocks with socks in order to appear hip and relatable to my students.

Me You look like my grandfather.

Professor SUCCESS.

V

Professor If anybody needs me, I've posted office hours on Monday, Wednesday and Friday from 9-12.

Me I will make fun of you for this with my peers.

Professor Yes, but you will also show up during them the week before classes end, begging for extra credit to help your grade.

Me Touché, Professor. Touché.

VI

Professor You will email me your papers by midnight on October 10th.

Me My computer is going to break on October 10th.

Professor Make sure to back-up your files just in case. No excuses will be accepted.

Me My dog ate my hard drive.

Professor F.

Me I plan on crying.

Professor (begrudgingly) Fine. You have 48 hours. (pause) I was once like you, you know.

VII

Professor Participation will account for 30% of your grade.

Me Bullsh.

Professor Truth. I will not keep track of your participation.

Me This class rules!

Professor Here is a Werther's Original for coming to class today.

Me Yes.

VIII

Professor I do not believe in tests.

Me There is a God.

Professor TENURE!

Dr. Doom Finally Takes Over the World

By Patrick Cassels

DR. DOOM
Mr. Fantastic! You have received my demand for world domination. Are you prepared to call me master? Or shall I be forced to activate the Omega Turbine and cause further destruction to your beloved planet?

Mr. Fantastic appears on an enormous video monitor

MR. FANTASTIC
You're a madman, von Doom. A complete and utter madman! But... we accept your terms.

DR. DOOM
Insipid fool! Then your death await— Wha...? I am sorry, what did you say?

MR. FANTASTIC
You win, Dr. Doom. I've received unconditional surrenders from every sovereign nation on Earth. Congratulations, oh Exalted One!

DR. DOOM
Really? Wow. (Laughs nervously.) This is, um... it is just so unexpected. Unless— Of course! This is some clever ruse to buy time while you formulate a plan to stop me! A noble effort, but you are only delaying the inevitable!

MR. FANTASTIC
No, your Omnipotence. In fact, the militaries of the world are being flown to your Terror Zeppelin as we speak. They're part of your Extermination Force now. Obviously, the soldiers will require food and lodging.

DR. DOOM
Oh, I see. (Feigning confidence.) Yes, of course. Then I... I have done it... Victory is mine. This is totally what I wanted.

MR. FANTASTIC
I've also taken the liberty of delivering you a list of the agricultural and socio-economic statistics of the Northern Hemisphere.

DR. DOOM
What?

MR. FANTASTIC
Yes, I thought it might be too much to send you all the world economies on your first day, Lord Doom. After all, you are only human—and ten percent demon, of course! (Laughs.)

DR. DOOM
Right.

MR. FANTASTIC
The most pressing issues, as you probably know, are the summer harvests in East Asia, which are imperative in maintaining the migratory patterns of most winged... Well, it's all in volume 28, my Lord. In the meantime, have you any decrees to make?

DR. DOOM
Um... Well yes, actually. (Reads from crumpled napkin.) I... um... I demand a 1500-foot golden statue of me, Victor von Doom, be built. In this statue I shall be riding a scorpion. And holding one of those two-necked guitars used by James Page of Led Zepplin.

MR. FANTASTIC
I'm sorry, Lord Jaguar, but weren't all Earth's precious metals irradiated by your Omega Turbine?

DR. DOOM
Oh, right. Well, I guess it could be carved out of stone.

MR. FANTASTIC
Wow! So then you've discovered a way of returning the world's skilled laborers from the Phantom Zone?

DR. DOOM
Curses! This meeting is over! A television program shall help me relax.

Doom turns on the TV. Every channel is static.

DR. DOOM
What is wrong with this device?

MR. FANTASTIC
I guess you're still using all those stolen satellites for your death ray, huh?

DR. DOOM
Yes.

The electricity goes out.

DR. DOOM
(Pause.) I did not think this through.

Sleeping Routine the Night Before Finals

By Jeff Rosenberg

Let's get one thing straight — we're all procrastinators. It's practically the only thing that unites the races, sexes and species in the animal kingdom. And it seems that everyone has a similar method for studying the night leading up to a final.

Before you even crack that textbook open for the first time (and possibly tear the plastic wrap off) it's safe to pray to the Finals God. Without his mercy we have nothing to live for. This is a moment of desperation and even though you don't believe in God, you need him by your side right now. Remember, there are no atheists in foxholes.

Whoa, ok wow there's a lot of text in this book and slim to nil pics. Did NOT see that coming. And what's with the font-size and margins? Are they trying to pack as much information as they can on this page? Jesus Fuc— sorry God, didn't mean that. Please let me pass. It's just— haha— ok I just feel a little light-headed is all. Maybe rocking back and forth will help.

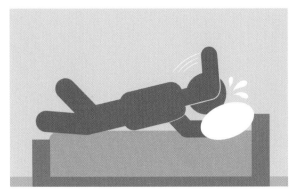

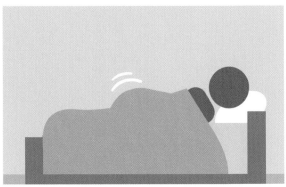

NO! NO! NO! NO! NO! Rocking back and forth did not help. You know what? I need a break. NO! No breaks. Not yet. Okay, there's no way I can read the entire book. Maybe I'll just skim. Look for keywords and just get the jist of it. That's all these tests are anyway— recall. But geez 32 pages in a chapter that's a lot of skimming. Ok, getting a little dizzy. Lying down.

Ok, chapter skimming done. Reward yourself.

That's how to get things done baby!! You do some chapter skimming. You get a reward. Phew, little tired from that though. OK, man up man up. Gotta ride the Bull. We knew we'd have to do this. Let's just raid the roomie's fridge right quick. OK OK OK LIQUID CANDY ENERGY LET'S GET PUMPED. 1 out of 6 chapters skimmed. LET'S GO BABY!

FUCK FUCK FUCK FUCK FUCK. I can't do this. Next chapter was 42 pages!!! HAHA WHAT IS THAT?! I CAN'T TAKE THIS. I'M NOT READY. FUCK FUCK FUCK. THINK. FUCK. OK, WE'RE DEFINITELY NOT TAKING IT. IT'S TOO HARD. HAHA I'LL JUST BRUISE MYSELF UP A LIT-TLE. CAN'T LET A CRIPPLE TAKE A FINAL?!? THAT'S INHUMANE. I CAN DO THIS. I CAN DO THIS. I LOVE YOU MOM. I CAN DO THIS.

Repeat tomorrow night for next final, right after watching a movie. Or two. And checking Facebook really quick.

I can't do this. Fuck.

Porn-O-Vision

Things look a little different when you've been watching a lot of porn...

PORN　　　　　　　　　　　　　**REALITY**

PORN REALITY

The 8 People You See Outside Every College Party

By Susanna Wolff

The Waiter

Hey, yeah, just waiting for my friends. Yep. Man, where are they? They said 11:15 and it is 11:28 right now. 11:29! If they don't get here soon, we're going to miss all the beer. Maybe I'll just go in alone and get a cup now. Nah. It would be really lame to show up to a party alone. I'll just stand out here and stare at my phone. I'll put it back in my pocket every once in a while so I can take it out again with an indignant look, this way everyone clearly knows that I'm waiting for friends and not just standing alone outside a party like an a-hole. 11:31!

The Smoker

Hey, can I bum a light? And a cigarette? I try to only smoke when I drink, not just because I think it's healthier, but because it means I never have to buy cigarettes. Ahhh. Let me lean back against this recycling bin full of puke while I exhale. Look how cool I look. Are you looking? Of course you are. Watch me spit. Oh yeah. I started smoking two months ago just so I'd have an excuse to go outside when I had to fart while I was at the library. Ahhh. So cool.

The Texter

Oh, hey, attractive smoker I was was just trying to talk to inside the party. Fancy meeting you out here! You said you were going out for a cigarette? I must have missed that. I'm out here because I have to send a really important text and the service in there is like yikes. Only 4 bars. Stupid Alltel. Do you use Alltel? No? No one uses Alltel? Ha! You're so right. I'm def gonna change providers. You're really cool and smart. Anyway, now that I've got you away from your protective friends, I'm going to try to make out with you.

The Fighting Couple

Yes, we have to do this right here! I'm a cunt! I'm an asshole! That's all anyone else at this party knows about us! We're irrationally jealous even though we're both cheating on each other and we're definitely going to break up for the summer! We are? Well, fuck you! Fuck you! We're not going to break up tonight, though, because one of us has a dorm room that's really nearby this party! We're going to apologize without meaning it so we can carry on with this vapid relationship until the next time either of us has a drink or goes on Facebook and the fighting starts again.

The Drunk Dialer

Hey, baby. I miss you so much. I juss had to call you righ' now. We were craze to break up siss years ago. N'one undessands m'li you do. I said, no one unnersands me like you do. Who's zat with you? Jake? Who's Jake? Are you fucking him?! Of course it's my business, you slut. Well guess what? I'm at a party right now. A really cool party at a much cooler college than yours. "Yale University," more like "Fail University." Hello? Hello? Ugh... Call home. Home! Hey, mom. I miss you so much. I juss had to call you righ' now.

The Mess

I'm nod druk. I'm nod! I'm juss really tired. Less sit down righ' here. I'm gonna trip an end up sitting anyway. I do this every weekend. Isnit weird tha I still have friends? Din Madd look hot? Matt. Thas a hard name. Where's my phone?! Oh, righ' righ' I'm holding it. I can prolly only get away with being this much of a mess fer like one more semesser before all my dresses have grass stains and I starda getta double chin like my mom. Less sit down righ' here. Less sit. Where's my phone?! I'm nod druk.

The Mess' Friend

Why am I always nice enough to drag her home every weekend? Right, because I'm her fat friend. Come on, Ashleigh, stop sitting down. Jesus! For some reason I still think that hanging out with you is going to make me popular on my own, but it won't! Get up. Somehow, even though I'm not the one lying in an old pizza box, I still look less attractive to that guy who's whimpering on the phone to his mom over there. Whatever. If he tries to talk to her I'll just be super bitchy. It's all part of the fat friend job.

The Guy Who Wants To Goooo

Ugh, this is the reason my friends don't like inviting me to partiiiies. I started whining about how loud and crowded it was almost immediately, but I refuse to just leave by myself. Instead, I'm going to stand out here and drink this watery, putrid excuse for beer and make annoyed gestures at my friends through the window. I can't believe they like this lame party. This is the worst party ever, but for the rest of the week, whenever someone asks what I did over the weekend, I'm going tell them about how I went to the coolest party ever. Ugh, it's 11:31. I'm missing the SNL monologue. Eh, it's not like that show's even good anymore.

233

What Are You Majoring In?

By Caldwell Tanner

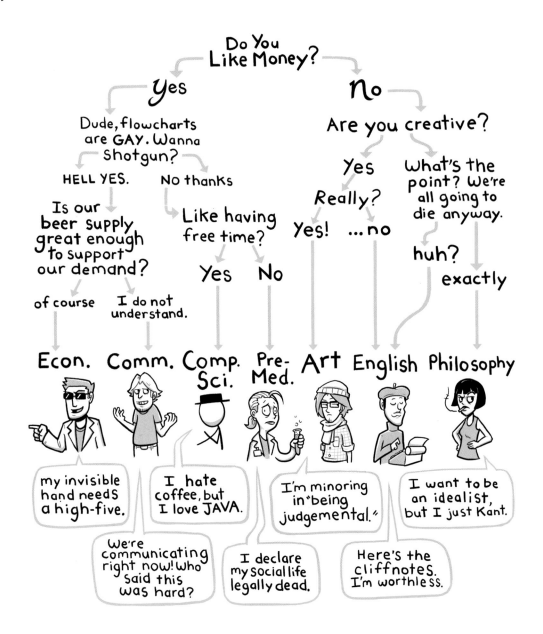

The Truth About Crop Circles

By Owen Parsons

The New Testament

By Lev Novak

God Hey Jews.

Jews Hey.

God So listen, guys, I'm thinking we go in a different direction with this whole religion.

Jews What?

God You know, do a non-gritty reboot. Same God taste, new God packaging. That sort of thing.

Jews We don't follow.

God Okay, work with me here, guys. Remember the whole "angry God" thing?

Jews Vividly.

God Where I killed a whole bunch of you and—

Jews Yeah.

God And forty years in the—

Jews We remember that.

God Not to mention Robo-Hitler. Yikes.

Jews Wait, what?

God Whoops, forget I said that. "Spoiler Alert," am I right?

Jews ...

God Anyway, we're going to re-work this whole "God" thing. For example, kid-friendly is big these days in religion.

Jews So, like...?

God For example, I'm super chill now, for some reason. Plus there's a heaven. Oh, and this is Jesus. He's my son, and he's God too, or something. It's complicated, ok?

Jesus Yo.

Jews I think we'll stick with the old one here.

God Look, I love the brand loyalty, Jews, I really do. But this whole "God" thing isn't playing to the right demographics. Jesus is a hip, young God, you know, for the whole "A.D." generations.

Jesus Surf's up, dudes!

God Ha, that Jesus. What a character, right? This is going to play huge in Rome...

Jews This...goes against everything you've ever told us.

God No it doesn't, so just shut up. Also, Jesus, you're going to die.

Jesus What? I thought I was your son! Or God. Or both!

God Look, this is just complicated, okay Jesus? Besides, you totally return when you fight the Devil.

Jews Who?

God Right, he's another new character. He's like an evil God. Plot twist, right? We're arch enemies.

Jesus Why would you make your own arch-enemy? That's really stupid.

God Shut up, Jesus. And what would you know? You're made of bread and wine.

Jesus What? Why?

God Sponsorships, alright? New testaments aren't cheap.

Jews I'm sorry, this is just way too different. Is this your fan-fiction or something?

God Of course not. This is the logical progression of Judaism which I planned all along. Like when I made all those references to a lamb.

236

Jews You made, like, five.

God Well, they were all about Jesus. Fore-shadowing. Um, I guess. So there.

Jews Couldn't you have been clearer then?

God I work in mysterious ways, okay? Look, just go with it guys. I worked really hard on this. And come on, you totally owe me for the whole "creation" thing anyway.

(pause)

Most Jews

Well, I guess we could.

God Awesome! "Most Jews," aka "New Christians"—

New Christians

We're what now?

God You won't regret this guys. I have the whole thing planned perfectly.

Holy Ghost

Oooooooooh!

God ...

New Christians

...

God You're going to love it.

Cartoon University

By Patrick Merryman and Caldwell Tanner

Conversations That Led Up to the Invention of Facebook

By Clara Morris

I

Mark Hey, do you know anything about that cute girl from the bar?

Chris Not really, all I know is she's friends with Jared.

Mark Ah! I wish I could use that knowledge to learn more about her and see pictures of her and her friends!

Chris You could ask Jared, I guess.

Mark Well I don't really want to make it public that I'm trying to find out about her.

II

Chris Whoa, have you been at your computer all day? Didn't you have classes to go to?

Mark Yeah, I did. I'm so sick of this. I spent all day trying to get information on that girl from my econ class. I looked at her AIM profile to get her favorite quotes; Googled her and got some high school field hockey stats; looked through her Webshots page to see the kind of crowd she hangs out with—cuties, by the way—and I searched the university's clubs website to see if she registered with any. Man, all this research took forever! My life would be so much easier if there was one website that had all her information compiled in an easy to read format!

III

Chris Hey, what's up?

Mark I was thinking, there should be a way for me to alert everyone I've ever known when a good picture of me is taken.

IV

Chris Do you want to hit up the bars tonight?

Mark Dude, I want to, but I gotta stop spending money. I've been driving around following this girl I knew in middle school, you know, just to learn more about her before I actually talk to her. I'm having fun and learning a lot, but these gas prices! They're killing me! I'm going through a $30 tank a week; I can't afford this lifestyle! If only there was a way to stalk people without spending money on gas.

Chris You could walk?

Mark Yeah, I guess. But all that walking would really tire me out. I wish there was some way I could stalk people for free from a sitting down position.

V

Chris What are you up to?

Mark I'm making an Evite for my birthday party.

Chris That's cool. Evite's are pretty convenient, huh?

Mark Yeah, but I'm kinda bummed cuz only the people I'm inviting will see it. I want the people who aren't invited to see the evite, see who's coming, and read all the invited people's little comments about the event. Just so they know how much fun I'm excluding them from. Ah, in a perfect world.

VI

Chris How's it going?

Mark If I were in a relationship, I think I'd want to subtly alert everyone I've ever known of that fact.

Chris But what about when you break up? Would you want to tell people that?

Mark Yeah, definitely! I'd get so much sympathy attention. That would be the best! Why isn't there a forum for getting that kind of info out?!

The SMALL TALK Calendar

By Mike Bartlett

~every week~

S M T W T F S

"What did you do this weekend?"

"What are you doing this weekend?"

"What are you doing tonight?"

~month to month~

SEPTEMBER

"How was your summer?"

"Are you going to the game?"

OCTOBER

"How are your midterms going?"

"What are you being for Halloween?"

NOVEMBER

"What were you for Halloween?"

"Are you going home for Thanksgiving?"

DECEMBER

"How was your Thanksgiving?"

"Are you doing anything fun for Winter Break?"

"How are finals going?"

JANUARY

"How was your Winter Break?"

FEBRUARY

"How are your Midterms going?"

MARCH

"What are you doing for Spring Break?"

"How was your Spring Break?"

APRIL

"Can you believe this year is almost over?"

MAY

"How are your finals going?"

"What are you doing this Summer?"

SUMMER

"It's not the heat, it's the humidity."

Richie Rich Grows Up

By Patrick Cassels

Hello Mom and Dad,

It's me, your "Poor Little Rich Boy." Well, I'm not so little any more. But I am still rich. I'm 30 years old, sitting on a 10-figure trust fund just itching to be spent. And guess what: I do what I want, when I want. Just like I always said I would.

No parents. No rules. No consequences. $50 billion buys a lot of freedom, Dad. The kind of freedom I never knew in that Nazi regime you called a mansion. I've been living off a diet of cookie dough and Ring Pops for the last two months, and I've never felt more alive.

Sure, 80 percent of my teeth have rotted to the nerve, but who cares? It's not like I'm going to the dentist ever again. Or the doctor. In fact, I've bought the First Presbyterian Hospital and next week I'm blowing that needle-filled hell hole to the ground.

So screw you, Dad. I'm living out every fantasy I've ever had. Last week I finally built that wrestling ring in my bedroom. I pay bums $10 to let me give them Stone Cold Stunners. Turns out you were right about one thing though, Dad: It can break your neck.

And Mom, remember that time you caught me watching Die Hard and gave me some bullshit lecture on how dangerous guns could be? Remember? Now I own two unregistered AK-47s. And I use them. A lot. Fair warning, Bitchie Bitch: You are not off limits.

So Die Hard was too violent for me, huh? I'd hate to break it to you, but that shit looks like a fucking Disney film compared to the hardcore snuff I'm watching now. What kind of 16mm film do you think costs $2 million and is smuggled into the country via cargo vessel? I've seen genres you didn't even know existed, Mom. All of them erotic. None of them legal. Most of them Asian.

Anything goes at Rich mansion now. Anything. Say goodbye to those three years of potty training you wasted on me. Today I keep jars of my urine in a room bigger than most people's fucking houses. Yup, life's one big orgy of punishment-free manslaughter, illegal firearms, Eastern European women and, best of all, all the pancakes I can eat!

-Rich

Your Textbooks Rewritten As Erotic Novels

By Dan Gurewitch

1. His approach : her bed :: Japanese planes : Pearl Harbor

2. Her legs : his torso :: drawbridge : approaching seafaring vessel

3. His tongue : her Lotus flower :: Frodo : Middle-earth

4. Her orgasm : the neighbors :: Spring : hibernating bears

Slowly, Charles began to engage in the wild, passionate dance of digestion. He placed the burger in his mouth, masticating, masticating, faster now, his teeth tearing and crushing, his stomach churning with waves of pleasure. Various chemicals (acid, bile, enzymes and water) caressed the complex molecules, their firm yet tender touch reducing them to simple structures blind with desire. His nutrients moaned, submissive slaves to osmosis. Finally, in a volcanic release that shook his naked body, Charles defecated.

Nietzsche thrusted deeper and deeper between the supple legs of Simone de Beauvoir, yelling, "Who's your ubermensch?" Simone lost herself in the heavenly unison of their eager bodies, moaning, "Oh, God…oh, God!" as, despite her post-feminist ideology, she made herself flesh under the dominance of the Other's gaze. "God is DEAD!" screamed Nietzsche, his fingernails digging into her existentialist buttocks as they reached the disillusioning and wholly temporary ecstasy of orgasm. Nietzsche rolled over and lit up a cigarette. "Thus poked Zarathustra," he said.

In 1864, General Sherman marched to the sea, his rifle throbbing and erect. His man-sweat smelling of gunpowder and lust, he penetrated the South… deeper… deeper still. "Scorch my earth," moaned the South. Sherman's loins quivered as he killed field after field of luscious, moist livestock, his body shaking with the unspeakable pleasure of destroying the civilian infrastructure.

Their love sounded so good on paper, but now Marx and Engels were faced with the reality of bare flesh pressed against bare flesh, their proletarian members waiting to be emancipated from the shackles of their capitalist trousers. Their role-playing grew vicious – "Exploit me! Alienate me!" screamed Engels as he rejected feudalist and capitalist ideals, surrendering himself to Marx's bourgeois tyranny. At last, their love wasn't just theoretical – they stared into each others' eyes as the workers of their world united. Almost immediately afterward, they collapsed.

The melting ice trickled down the mountain's spine, at once cool and warm, the sensation causing the mountain to gasp sublimated water vapor. The sun beat down on the trees, and the trees reveled in the sweet intersection of pain and pleasure, beginning to sweat. "Evapotranspiration," whispered the sun, soft yet in control. The trees' sweat droplets condensed, clinging to each other in a hazy airborne dance of lust. The clouds grew in the sky, trembling slightly, the tension unbearable – then, with a roar, they precipitated. Mother Nature got up to clean herself off, ready to start again.

That night, Brandon went down on Juliette N times. He let NH be the number of times she climaxed, realizing that he could, for any N, consider the ratio NH/N. As N grew larger and larger, faster and faster, Brandon was able to "define" the probability Pr(H) as Juliette's sexual "limit." As N approached infinity in the equation $Pr(H) = \lim_{N \to \infty} (NH/N)$, Juliette's loins melted into his like the wax of a century-lost love candle.

…and she knew that after where she'd gone, she could never go back.

The end.

God is high like a kite...literally 'cuz I'm in da SKY

 God is just sittin' around bein' omnipotent... hit me up on IM

 God remembered no one's here. Nevamind.

 God is borrrrrrrrrrrrred lol

God created a new group

Light
Common Interest – Religion & Spirituality

God created a new group

Earth
Geography – Places

God created a new group

Eden
Geography – Neighborhoods

Adam is F1RST!

God and Adam are now friends.

God wrote on **Adam's wall**.
"yo man, hows it hangin?"

Adam wrote on **God's wall**.
kinda lonely. nbd. maybe make something I can stick this thing between my legs in? I think I want to do that.

Adam and Eve are in a relationship.

God wrote a new note

Some rules 4 the garden
No shirt, no shoes, no sin, NO PROBLEM!!!1!
Stay away from the apples. Seriously.
Go to the note...

God added a new photo album.

Fake Dinosaur Fossils
500 photos

Adam hahaha. yeah right like anyone will ever believe these weird things existed.

Eve psh yeah. you made the arms way too small on that one.

The Serpent FAIL

247

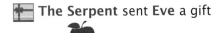 **The Serpent** sent **Eve** a gift

"Enjoy!"
5 minutes ago

> **God** WTF?! O come on u cannot be serious
> 5 minutes ago

Adam and **Eve** added application **Shame**

 Adam and **Eve** left the group **Garden of Eden**

 It's complicated between **Adam** and **Eve**

Adam and **Eve** joined the group **The Harsh Reality of the Outside World**

 Adam created the group **If Two People Join This Group, My Lord Will Let Me Back Into Paradise!!!** Organizations – Religious organizations
13 minutes ago

> **God**"Uhhhhh… or NOT. go beget some kids or sumthin."
> 5 minutes ago

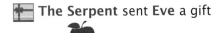 **God** sent **Eve** a gift

"it's the pain of childbirth! Hope that apple was worth it. btw ur just a rib. Probably why Adam wanted to BONE ya! hahaha ha lol"
13 minutes ago

248

God sent **Adam** a gift

"hard labor for ya, bra. FOREVER. FOORR–EVERRRR. Haha squints. you'll figure out what that means in a few million years"

Cain and **Abel** joined the group The Human Race

Abel created a new album

Best Brothers Ever (Literally, We're The Only Ones So We Are By Definition The Best)

3 photos

 Cain oh I am so gonna murder u
3 minutes ago

Abel "murder" me? what the heck does 'murder' mean?
2 minutes ago

 Abel has left the group **The Human Race**

God is thinking He probably should have taken that week off.

If I Acted Like My Computer Did on the First Day of Work

By Jesse Eisemann

Boss Jesse!

Me Sorry boss, fell asleep.

Boss I got up to get coffee. That's an absurd amount of time to fall asleep in. Did you get my mail yet?

Me Yeah boss, got it in .2 seconds!

Boss I asked for this 20 minutes ago.

Me That's improbable.

Boss It happened. This is all my mail?

Me Results 1-5. Here, give me those back and I'll show you the next 5.

Boss I'd like to just look at them all at the same time. And please stop playing with that hourglass.

Me Sorry.

Boss Also, I see you didn't print the memo I asked you to.

Me Yeah about that...Are you sure you want to print it?

Boss Wholly and completely.

Me Okay, it's just that—you didn't use real words. Look at this one.

Boss That's my name.

Me Right, here we go then. Hold on it appears you're not connected to the internet.

Boss What? Here, let me—

Me Hey, your network configuration has changed!

Boss Thank you, that was me changing it manually. Listen, when you're done printing can you find "gr-

Me "Granny trannie panties?"

Boss ..."green computing solutions." That must be left over from your old boss. I'm gonna need you to forget everything he ever asked of you. Can you do that?

Me ...

Boss Jesse? Jesse put the hourglass down. Okay this isn't working out. You're unresponsive; I'm going to have to-

Me You can't fire me! (storms out of office)

Secretary Sir, Jesse quit unexpectedly.

Adventurous Adventures

By Caldwell Tanner

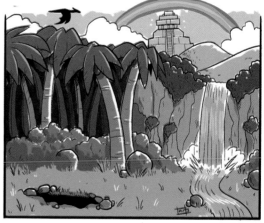

The Universal Freshman Class Syllabus

By Dan Gurewitch

Deceptively Difficult Astronomy
M, T, W, Th, F @8:00 AM
Lab: Sat. 5:30AM-12:30PM
Professor: Rigladesh Manaramayani

About the Professor:
Widely known as India's fastest talking scientist, Prof. Manaramayani moved to the United States earlier this morning to seek a medical cure for his speech impediment.

Class Objectives:
- Attain a swift and comprehensive hatred of subject matter
- Improve doodling and crossword puzzle aptitude
- Class should be a mutual learning experience. Just as I am responsible for teaching you astronomy, you will be responsible for teaching me English.

Required Textbooks:
- Astronomy: A Physical Perspective
- Our Evolving Universe
- Introduction to Optical Stellar Interferometry Astrophysical Fluid Dynamics
- Goodnight Moon
- The Epic of Gilgamesh
- Mirriam-Webster Hindi-English Dictionary

Attendance:
I will be reading directly from my PowerPoint slides, then emailing you the exact slides that I read in class, except on days that you miss class.

Quizzes:
There will be quizzes literally (a) all of the time, (b) every single day, (c) all of the above. Explain your answer.

Exams/Grading:
Exams will be hyper-comprehensive, meaning you will be expected to have full and complete knowledge of all fields of science. Each of the four exams will count for the full 100% of your grade.

Labs:
Your seven-hour Saturday morning lab class will be divided into four groups of four. The hot girl will not be in your group. The four hot girls will be in the same group.

Please stop looking at that group.

Meanwhile on an Airplane...

By Amir Blumenfeld

A man clutches his chest and keels over into the aisle.

Stewardess
OH MY GOD! IS THERE A DOCTOR ON THIS FLIGHT?

Doctor
I'm a doctor. Step aside.

Stewardess
Is there anything you need?

Doctor
Yes. Is there a nurse on this flight?!

Nurse
I'm a nurse.

Doctor
Dammit, there's no time. He stopped breathing and if we don't act fast, we'll lose him.

Nurse
He's gone.

Stewardess
What? How?

Nurse
Is there a pathologist on this flight?!

Pathologist
I'm a pathologist.

Doctor
Any ideas?

Pathologist
From the way he fell it looked like a myocardial infarction. We won't know for sure until the results come back from the lab.

Stewardess
Wanna dumb that down for me? I'm not a rocket scientist.

Rocket Scientist
A heart attack.

Stewardess
Wow. A rocket scientist, a doctor, a nurse, a pathologist. What are the odds?!

Statistician
Roughly 1 in 140,000.

Doctor
Is there a pilot on this flight?

Pilot
Of course.

Doctor
We're going to need to turn this plane around.

Pilot
What about the career fair?

Career Fair Coordinator
I guess that can wait.

253

Party Time!!!

To the guests of **Freddy's Fantastic Finals Farty**

Fred Hollingsworth April 2 at 9:22am
Woah!! Can you believe my "Fantastic Finals" party is already only two months away?

I know some of you like to "play it cool" and respond at the last minute, but it's super-important I have an accurate guest count, so I'm setting up a firm RSVP deadline of April 30th, 4:00pm EST. No exeptions!
Also, if you haven't already, check out the Google Doc I sent out–it has slots to sign up to bring food, dessert items, recommended drink mixers, etc.

Can't wait!!!!!

–Fred a.k.a. "Freddy" Hollingsworth

Fred Hollingsworth April 30 at 2:04pm
Hey! Not sure if you all saw the last message, but the deadline to RSVP is in two hours, and you should have signed up last Tuesday to bring food/drinks.

Don't freak out, though–I've extended the deadline until THIS FRIDAY! (Tomorrow, FYI.)
Looking forward to your RVSP's. Tweet at me with any questions @FreddyFantaztic Be sure to get your party pants ironed, this is going to be one shindig you don't want to miss.

–Fred "The Fredmeister" Hollingsworth

Fred Hollingsworth May 1 at 5:23
Sorry to get serious for a moment, but whoever altered the Goodle Doc to in-clude (quoting here) "Freddy's pussy juice," "deer cum," and "you're a gaytard," please identify yourself so I can remove you from the approved list of invitees. I'm all for having a good time, but not at the expense of others. Cool?

Thanks for you're understanding.

–The One and Only Fredinator

Fred Hollingsworth May 2 at 5:27
*your

–F

Fred Hollingsworth May 30 at 11:22pm
OK. Look. I know Facebook includes a "Maybe" RSVP, but that's not really a
FUCKING ANSWER, is it?? You're seriously fucking better off not even replying
at all. I just wanted to throw a party where people could come have fun and not
give the same guy five dollars for a cup three times in a row, even though he
clearly fucking recognizes me. So yeah...Let's be adults about this, OK?

–Frederick "Not Pissed, Just Frustrated" Hollingsworth

Fred Hollingsworth May 31 at 10:23am
Guys–

I want to apologize upfront for the tone of last night's message. Just because
Mom and I are having some "territory" issues, that's no reason to take it out on
you guys.

Definitely don't let it keep you from coming and having a kick–ass time, and I
hope to see you all respond "Oh Hell Yeah." (JK! Not a real option, but it would
better than "Maybe." Seriously, let me know.)

Peace out,

–Frederick "Face Palming Myself Right Now" Hollingsworth

Trevor Richards June 2 at 3:21pm
STFU fag

Fred Hollingsworth June 2 3:24
LOL yeah right!

Party's in three days, guys. Not to going to name any names, but still missing some pretty major RSVPs. Seriously, BBM me with any questions ASAP, my PIN 31823EEC.

Get redy to shake it like a Polaroid picture,

–Fred "Force Five" Hollingsworth

Fred Hollingsworth June 6 at 11:57am
Wow! EPIC party! SO MUCH FUN!

Sorry you guys who came couldn't stay longer, but at least you got some beers for the road. Also, if you borrowed anything, please return it at your earliest convenience...I really need my deposit back on that keg.

To those of you who missed the "Party Donations" shoebox, that's totally cool, you can just hit me back via PayPal or personal check. Sooner the better, checking account is mucho overdrawn right now.

Final note: If anybody's seen my laptop, please return it to me right away. Writing this from the library, not sure they'll let me stay here much longer.

Party buds 4 eva,

–F-bomb

The Imagination of Wendell Blatt As He Goes Swimming

By Jake Hurwitz

A guy and girl lifeguard at the public pool:

Guy Look at that fat kid that just jumped in the pool!

Girl That's Wendall Blatt you gay idiot. How can you even tell he's fat? He's wearing a big t-shirt.

Guy Trust me, he's fat as shit. Why else would he try to hide his body under a t-shirt?

Girl Duh, it's more comfortable. I wish I could swim in a t-shirt, but my boobs are too big.

Guy Doesn't my nose look retarded with this sunblock and aren't my glasses too big for my pea sized head?

Girl Yes.

Guy I'm a gay ass loser and now I'm going to blow my whistle at Wendell and tell him to stop hanging on the lane line.

Girl He's not hanging on the lane line, he's resting for one second, relax. You don't know how hard it is to swim in a soaking wet oversized t-shirt.

Guy Oh my God the water is changing colors near him. I think he's peeing. Look he's looking around to see if anyone is noticing.

Girl So what? The pool is freezing. I pee in the pool all the time. God my nipples are hard.

Guy Isn't that Wendell's mom by the pool flirting with those high school kids?

Girl Yeah right. She's just talking to them.

Guy I heard sometimes they come over to her house.

Girl Shut up, okay? Wendell's dad is probably moving back in anyway.

Guy Sorry. I should have known. I'm such a huge loser.

Girl I know

Begins taking off her bathing suit.

Guy What are you doing?

Girl What does it look like I'm doing? I'm getting naked and I'm gonna go under water and blow Wendell.

Guy What if someone sees you?

Girl I hope everyone sees me. Then maybe they'll realize how awesome Wendell is. Oh and one more thing: Sugar Ray is still cool.

Guy I know.

REALITY

Guy Hey, Cindy, can you come here?

Girl What's up?

Guy I think that fat kid in the t-shirt is sticking his dick in one of the jets again. You wanna get that?

Girl Yeah.

257

Drunk-O-Vision IV

Things look a little different when you're drunk...

REALITY

DRUNK

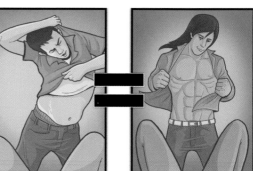

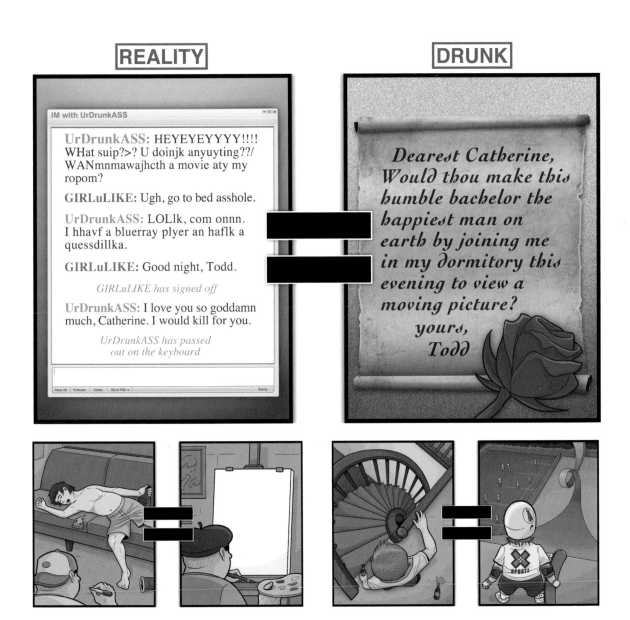

REALITY

IM with UrDrunkASS

UrDrunkASS: HEYEYEYYYY!!!!
WHat suip?>? U doinjk anyuyting??/
WANmnmawajhcth a movie aty my
ropom?

GIRLuLIKE: Ugh, go to bed asshole.

UrDrunkASS: LOLlk, com onnn.
I hhavf a bluerray plyer an haflk a
quessdillka.

GIRLuLIKE: Good night, Todd.

GIRLuLIKE has signed off

UrDrunkASS: I love you so goddamn
much, Catherine. I would kill for you.

*UrDrunkASS has passed
out on the keyboard*

DRUNK

*Dearest Catherine,
Would thou make this
humble bachelor the
happiest man on
earth by joining me
in my dormitory this
evening to view a
moving picture?
yours,
Todd*

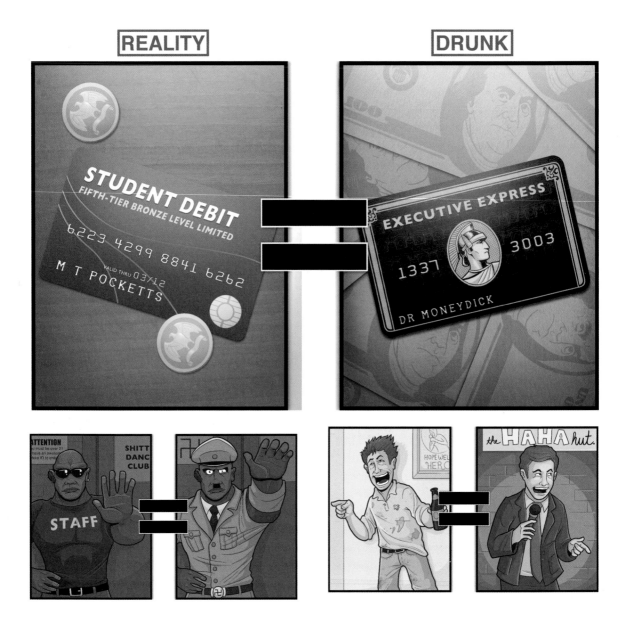

260

Party Invitation

By Patrick Cassels

Ladies, gentlemen,
party animals young and old
your day has arrived.
Tonight, 10 pm at dormitory complex B-18,
it's BOOZE-TOPIA 2008!!!
What better way to kick off the spring semester than a lawless, hedonistic orgy of alcohol, music, and an "anything goes" atmosphere?

Quick FYI, this party is BYOB- "Bring Your Own Booze." (Duh!)

I've spent the last four years planning this liquor-filled, lascivious soiree, and tonight you boozers will see just what kind of drunken tomfoolery you're all capable of. Leave your inhibitions at home, amigos! (Do not, however, leave your alcohol at home, since, again, this is a BYOB affair. I cannot stress this fact enough.)

One quick Booze-topia 2008 update: It turns out alcohol is not, in fact, permitted in the dormitories after all. This is a minor oversight. I tried slipping our building's Ukrainian security guard a cool $100 to "look the other way," but this seemed only to provoke enraged screams from Krzysztof in his native Eastern tongue, which wouldn't have bothered me if he had returned the 100 dollars. Speaking of which, another Booze-topia update: There will be a $5 cover for tonight's "anything goes" mixer!!!

Don't fret about this "prohibition" business. I've taken steps to ensure the nectar shall flow tonight, and flow well. Enclosed with this invitation you'll find a rinsed-out jar of Hellmann's mayonnaise. Those of you looking to get rightly HAMMERED! just fill this "party jar" with the drink of your choice, seal the lid, and casually stroll past the building's front desk like an innocent, campus-code-obeying student returing from the grocery store.

Of course, no food of any kind will actually be permitted tonight. My roommate, Huang, who is visiting his grandparents in Beijing this week, is very particular about crumbs on the carpet. So please, no food. Or shoes. Or gum. Just FUN!!! (And 5 dollars.)

A final Booze-topia update: You may want to re-rinse out the enclosed mayonnaise jar. The water pressure in my room is incredibly weak. Please make sure you "do your business" before entering this "party zone!"

And with that, comrades, I will bid you a fine farewell until the degradation begins at 10!!! I, for one, plan on downing at least 3 mayo jars of Coors Light. Anyone think they can top that? Well, you can't: I'm imposing a 3 jar limit to avoid suspicion. Please respect the guidelines of my "anything goes" BONANZA!

Yearbook Notes From Martin Hoppler, Extremely Honest High School Senior

By Dan Gurewitch

DEREK—
I'LL NEVER FORGET HOW MUCH FUN WE HAD IN "FIDDLER ON THE ROOF." DIEDLE-DEEDLE-DEEDLE-DUM! NOW, LET'S FACE FACTS: YOU'RE GAY. LITERALLY EVERYBODY KNOWS THIS BUT YOU. I WANT YOU TO KNOW THAT WHEN YOU DISCOVER IT FOR YOURSELF, I WILL SUPPORT YOU 100%. TAKE THIS OPPORTUNITY TO GREASE THE GEARS OF SELF-REFLECTION, THOUGH. YOU ARE NO-HOLDS-BARRED, IT'S-NOT-JUST-EXPERIMENTING, NEIL PATRICK HARRIS, "BIRDCAGE" GAY.

—MARTIN

DIANA—
YOUR THONG-PROTRUDING BUTTOCKS ALWAYS MADE MRS. FLANDERJAN'S 3RD PERIOD HISTORY CLASS MORE FUN. SOMETIMES I WOULD MISS ENTIRE CHAPTERS OF NOTES JUST IMAGINING WHAT IT WOULD FEEL LIKE TO LAY MY HEAD UPON ONE OF YOUR BUTTOCKS. ONE TIME, I WROTE AN ENTIRE IN-CLASS ESSAY ABOUT BOSS TWEED WITHOUT TAKING MY EYES OFF OF YOUR BUTTOCKS. I KNOW NEXT TO NOTHING ABOUT YOU! AS I FINISH WRITING THIS SENTENCE, I'VE ALREADY FORGOTTEN YOUR NAME.

—MARTIN

KEVIN, WE'VE BEEN BEST FRIENDS SINCE 2ND GRADE. WE'RE LIKE BROTHERS. CAN YOU BELIEVE THAT WHEN WE HANG OUT NEXT SUMMER, WE'LL IMMEDIATELY REALIZE THAT WE NO LONGER HAVE ANYTHING IN COMMON? I'LL HAVE AN INTERNSHIP AT MORGAN STANLEY, AND YOU'LL WANT TO "SMOKE A DOOB" IN THE PARK BEHIND WAFFLE HOUSE AND TALK ABOUT WHICH OF OUR MIDDLE SCHOOL TEACHERS YOU'D BUTT-BONE. 12 YEARS OF FRIENDSHIP, ERASED!

HAVE A GR8 SUMMER

—MARTIN

SARAH—
OUR RELATIONSHIP HAS MEANT
EVERYTHING TO ME. YOU WERE
MY FIRST KISS. MY FIRST, WELL... (!)

THAT SAID, <u>COLLEGE!</u> I'M
GOING TO BREAK UP WITH YOU IN AUGUST.
I'D LIKE TO THANK YOU IN ADVANCE
FOR YOUR PATIENCE AS I WILL BE
CALLING YOU REPEATEDLY AFTER
OUR BREAKUP TO EASE THE DULL
ACHE OF LONLINESS, AND FOR ALL
THE TIMES I WILL BE MASTURBATING
TO YOUR YEARBOOK PICTURE, MY
FOREHEAD VEIN BULGING WITH
REGRET.
          —MARTIN

MR JACOBS — I KNOW, "CALL YOU GARY"—
WHEN I HAD YOU FOR ENGLISH
FRESHMAN YEAR, I THOUGHT YOU
WERE THE COOLEST GUY ON THE
PLANET. YOU SAID THE WORD "ASS"
AND PLAYED MR. JONES ON YOUR
GUITAR AND QUOTED "MONTY PYTHON
AND THE HOLY GRAIL" Ni! BUT
YOU SEE ~~MR. JAC~~ GARY, AGE HAS
TAUGHT ME THAT FAILED STAND-UP
COMEDIANS AREN'T ROLE MODELS.
TAKE CARE! I CAN'T SEE MYSELF
COMING BACK TO VISIT. OUR LIVES
WILL ABSOLUTELY NEVER CROSS
AGAIN, IN ANY CONTEXT.

          —MARTIN

HEY TONY!
I HOPE YOU HAVE A LOT OF FUN
AT PENN STATE NEXT YEAR.
WE'RE REAL GOOD BUDS, AND OVER
THE PAST FOUR YEARS, WE'VE
BORROWED A LOT OF MONEY FROM
EACH OTHER FOR SNACKS AT
LUNCH. I'VE ACTUALLY BEEN
KEEPING TABS, AND THE TOTAL
COMES TO $46.25 IN MY
FAVOR. IF YOU COULD GET THAT
TO ME BEFORE THE END OF
FIFTH PERIOD, THAT WOULD
BE GREAT. GO WILDCATS!

          —MARTIN

Author Biographies

Amir Blumenfeld is a senior writer for CollegeHumor, where he co-authored *The CollegeHumor Guide to College* and *Faking It: How to Seem Like a Better Person Without Actually Improving Yourself*. He has written for The CollegeHumor Show and Pranked on MTV as well as several hundred episodes of the web series "Jake and Amir."

Andrew Bridgman is a contributing writer to CollegeHumor as well as Dorkly. He has written for McSweeney's Internet Tendency and was a featured playwright for the Louisville Specific Gravity Ensemble's Elevator Plays in 2007. He is currently working as an accountant in Manhattan.

Patrick Cassels joined CollegeHumor as a staff writer in 2007 and is co-host of the site's videogame show, "Bleep Bloop." He has written for Slate, McSweeney's Internet Tendency, Cracked, The Faster Times, and Kill Screen, and was published in McSweeney's humor collection, *Mountain Man Dance Moves*. He also edits a film blog, 10YearOldMovies.com.

Kevin Corrigan is a staff writer and editor for Collegehumor and Dorkly. He is also the co-creator of the popular Web series "Dinosaur Office" and was a headline contributor to *The Onion*.

Jon Gabrus is a comedian living in Brooklyn. He is a noted storyteller and improvisor, frequently seen at The Upright Citizens Brigade Theatre. As an actor, he has appeared on numerous television show as well as Internet shorts. His personal website can be found at Garbus.com.

Dan Gurewitch is a senior writer at College-Humor.com, where he has written hundreds of sketches. He was a head writer on The CollegeHumor Show, and is currently working on the screenplay for a CollegeHumor feature film. Outside of CollegeHumor, he has written numerous short films and contributed to *Newsweek*. He is a standup comedian and performs regularly at colleges around the country.

Steve Hofstetter is a standup comedian and CollegeHumor's first contributing writer. He has been featured on *The Late Show with Craig Ferguson*, *E! True Hollywood Stories*, *Comics Unleashed*, *Comedy All-Stars*, *Quite Frankly*, and *Countdown*. He performs 300 standup dates a year and has written for Sports Illustrated, The New York Times, Maxim, and the NHL.

Jake Hurwitz is a staff writer for CollegeHumor. He has written for McSweeney's Internet Tendency, Cosmopolitan, and makes up half the writing/acting/editing duo of the Web series, "Jake and Amir."

Casey Johnston is a frequent contributor to CollegeHumor. She has also written humor for Dorkly, McSweeney's Internet Tendency, The Rumpus, and *Mental_Floss*. She currently works as a technology journalist covering gaming, gadgets, science, and Apple for the website Ars Technica. Her journalistic work has also been featured on Wired and CNN.

Ben Joseph is the Creative Director of CollegeHumor Original Videos. Outside of CollegeHumor, he's had his work published by Cracked and McSweeney's Internet Tendency, and has written for the animated sketch show *MAD* and *The Simpsons*.

Patrick Merryman is a freelance writer from Poughkeepsie, New York. In addition to Collegehumor, he has written for YankeePot-Roast. Patrick currently attends Siena College.

Jason Michaels began writing for CollegeHumor while pursuing a Molecular and Cellular Biology degree at the University of Illinois. He is currently enrolled as a medical student in Illinois and continues to contribute articles to the website.

Clara Morris is a standup comedian who has performed extensively in New York City. She has also appeared in sketches with the group Olde English, one of which was nominated for an ECNY. Her work can be read at MrBellersNeighborhood.com. She currently lives in Atlanta, GA.

Brian Murphy has worked as a writer for CollegeHumor since 2008. He is the founding editor of Dorkly, a spinoff site focusing on videogames and gamer culture. He is the former humor editor for Rowan University's *Venue Magazine* and has been published in *Entertainment Weekly*'s "Must List." Brian is a writer for the animated series Dorkly Bits.

Lev Novak is a student at Tufts University and grew up in Newton, MA, in a family dedicated to both writing and comedy. Lev is a frequent contributor to CollegeHumor and Dorkly and is now working on his first novel.

Owen Parsons is a senior writer and illustrator for Dorkly and a staff writer for CollegeHumor. His work has been featured on McSweeney's Internet Tendency and in the *Stonefence Review* literary journal. He is a former editor of the Dartmouth *Jack-O-Lantern* humor magazine, as well as a contributing writer to MTV's Popzilla. He writes for the Upright Citizens Brigade Theatre's Maude Night, a monthly sketch comedy show.

Jeff Rosenberg began contributing to College-Humor in 2007 and is currently a staff writer. He is also CollegeHumor Image editor, responsible for curating the site's picture section.

Jeff Rubin is the Executive Editor of CollegeHumor. In addition to videos and articles for the website, he wrote for The CollegeHumor Show, co-authored *The CollegeHumor Guide to College*, and is the co-host and creator of the videogame talk show, "Bleep Bloop." He has appeared on VH1, G4, and ON Network's series *Play Value*. He is a standup comedian and performs regularly at colleges around the country.

Sarah Schneider is a Senior Writer for CollegeHumor. She has been writing for the site since 2005, and wrote for both *The CollegeHumor Guide to College* and MTV's *The CollegeHumor Show*. She is the co-creator of the CollegeHumor Web series "Full Benefits" and has written for the comedy news site SplitSider.com. She has also written for *Saturday Night Live*.

Streeter Seidell joined CollegeHumor in 2005 to co-author the site's first book, *The CollegeHumor Guide to College*, and is now Executive Editor of CollegeHumor Media. He was a writer on MTV's *The CollegeHumor Show* and *Pranked*. He has also written for *The New York Times*, *Wired*, McSweeney's Internet Tendency, *Men's Fitness*, *Metro New York*, and *Mental_Floss*.

Caldwell Tanner is the editorial illustrator for Collegehumor.com. Outside of illustrating the majority of CollegeHumor's articles, he maintains a site of his illustrations and writing at Loldwell.com.

Derek Walborn is a freelance artist working in both Rochester, NY, and Los Angeles, CA. He can be seen in the Oscar-nominated documentary *Exit Through the Gift Shop*. He stars in, co-writes and co-produces *Trails of Tarnation* with Jeff Stanin and Nicholas Gurewitch.

Alex Watt is a contributing writer for College-Humor. His work has also been featured on Dorkly, SportsPickle, McSweeney's Internet Tendency, and Yankee Pot Roast. Alex currently attends Hunter College where he studies English with a concentration in Creative Writing.

Susanna Wolff is a staff writer and Articles Editor at CollegeHumor. She began working at the site as an intern in 2007 and joined the staff full time in 2009.

David Young is a staff writer for CollegeHumor. He co-created the popular sketch comedy website JoeyandDavid.com and has created content for Warner Brothers and Fox. He's been named one of Variety's Top 10 Comics to Watch and performed at the prestigious HBO Aspen Comedy Festival. At CollegeHumor, he is the co-creator of the Web series "Full Benefits."